Capitalism

Other Books in the Current Controversies Series

Capitalism

Noël Merino, Book Editor

GREENHAVEN PRESS
A part of Gale, Cengage Learning

GALE
CENGAGE Learning™

Detroit • New York • San Francisco • New Haven, Conn • Waterville, Maine • London

Christine Nasso, *Publisher*
Elizabeth Des Chenes, *Managing Editor*

© 2010 Greenhaven Press, a part of Gale, Cengage Learning

Gale and Greenhaven Press are registered trademarks used herein under license.

For more information, contact:
Greenhaven Press
27500 Drake Rd.
Farmington Hills, MI 48331-3535
Or you can visit our Internet site at gale.cengage.com

For product information and technology assistance, contact us at

Gale Customer Support, 1-800-877-4253
For permission to use material from this text or product, submit all requests online at www.cengage.com/permissions

Further permissions questions can be emailed to permissionrequest@cengage.com

Articles in Greenhaven Press anthologies are often edited for length to meet page requirements. In addition, original titles of these works are changed to clearly present the main thesis and to explicitly indicate the author's opinion. Every effort is made to ensure that Greenhaven Press accurately reflects the original intent of the authors. Every effort has been made to trace the owners of copyrighted material.

Cover image © Joseph Sohm/Visions of America/Encylopedia/Corbis.

LIBRARY OF CONGRESS CATALOGING-IN-PUBLICATION DATA

Capitalism / Noël Merino, book editor.
    p. cm. -- (Current controversies)
    Includes bibliographical references and index.
    ISBN 978-0-7377-4699-0 (hardcover) -- ISBN 978-0-7377-4700-3 (pbk.)
    1. Capitalism. I. Merino, Noël.
    HB501.C242253 2010
    330.12'2--dc22

                                                    2009047743

Printed in the United States of America
1 2 3 4 5 6 7 14 13 12 11 10

Contents

Chapter 4: Does the Public Good Warrant Government Intervention in Capitalism?

**Yes: Government Intervention in the
Capitalist System Is Sometimes Warranted
for the Public Good**

Foreword

By definition, controversies are "discussions of questions in which opposing opinions clash" (Webster's Twentieth Century Dictionary Unabridged). Few would deny that controversies are a pervasive part of the human condition and exist on virtually every level of human enterprise. Controversies transpire between individuals and among groups, within nations and between nations. Controversies supply the grist necessary for progress by providing challenges and challengers to the status quo. They also create atmospheres where strife and warfare can flourish. A world without controversies would be a peaceful world; but it also would be, by and large, static and prosaic.

The Series' Purpose

The purpose of the Current Controversies series is to explore many of the social, political, and economic controversies dominating the national and international scenes today. Titles selected for inclusion in the series are highly focused and specific. For example, from the larger category of criminal justice, Current Controversies deals with specific topics such as police brutality, gun control, white collar crime, and others. The debates in Current Controversies also are presented in a useful, timeless fashion. Articles and book excerpts included in each title are selected if they contribute valuable, long-range ideas to the overall debate. And wherever possible, current information is enhanced with historical documents and other relevant materials. Thus, while individual titles are current in focus, every effort is made to ensure that they will not become quickly outdated. Books in the Current Controversies series will remain important resources for librarians, teachers, and students for many years.

In addition to keeping the titles focused and specific, great care is taken in the editorial format of each book in the series. Book introductions and chapter prefaces are offered to provide background material for readers. Chapters are organized around several key questions that are answered with diverse opinions representing all points on the political spectrum. Materials in each chapter include opinions in which authors clearly disagree as well as alternative opinions in which authors may agree on a broader issue but disagree on the possible solutions. In this way, the content of each volume in Current Controversies mirrors the mosaic of opinions encountered in society. Readers will quickly realize that there are many viable answers to these complex issues. By questioning each author's conclusions, students and casual readers can begin to develop the critical thinking skills so important to evaluating opinionated material.

Current Controversies is also ideal for controlled research. Each anthology in the series is composed of primary sources taken from a wide gamut of informational categories including periodicals, newspapers, books, U.S. and foreign government documents, and the publications of private and public organizations. Readers will find factual support for reports, debates, and research papers covering all areas of important issues. In addition, an annotated table of contents, an index, a book and periodical bibliography, and a list of organizations to contact are included in each book to expedite further research.

Perhaps more than ever before in history, people are confronted with diverse and contradictory information. During the Persian Gulf War, for example, the public was not only treated to minute-to-minute coverage of the war, it was also inundated with critiques of the coverage and countless analyses of the factors motivating U.S. involvement. Being able to sort through the plethora of opinions accompanying today's major issues, and to draw one's own conclusions, can be a complicated and frustrating struggle. It is the editors' hope that Current Controversies will help readers with this struggle.

Introduction

"Modern capitalists advocate a free market as a core component of capitalism."

Capitalism is an economic system based on the private, as opposed to public, ownership of capital. Capital is commonly defined as the means of production, such as land, factories, and technology, used to create goods or services. Under capitalism, any profits from business go to the private owners of businesses or, in the case of publicly held corporations, their shareholders. Workers, under capitalism, are paid wages for their employment, although workers do not necessarily have any ownership in the enterprise.

Capitalism can be starkly contrasted with communism, where the means of production and all property are owned in common by all. Under communism, any wealth created goes back into the common system for the benefit of all.

Modern capitalists advocate a free market as a core component of capitalism. One of the most influential supporters of the free market in recent decades was American economist Milton Friedman (1912–2006). Friedman opposed most forms of government intervention and regulation of the market. This particular brand of capitalism, which embraces the free market as a necessary component of a successful capitalist economy, is known as laissez-faire capitalism. 'Laissez-faire' comes from the French phrase meaning, "let it be." Proponents of laissez-faire capitalism believe that the markets should be allowed to work with very little or no government interference such as taxes, regulation, and public ownership. In *Capitalism and Freedom*, Friedman wrote, "A major source of objection to a free economy is precisely that it ... gives people what they want instead of what a particular group thinks they ought to want. Underlying most arguments against the free market is a lack of belief in freedom itself."[1]

Friedman and others justify laissez-faire capitalism by the idea that the marketplace will regulate itself by the force of "an invisible hand." The historical source of the idea of an invisible hand was eighteenth-century Scottish philosopher and economist Adam Smith (1723–1790). In his 1776 book, *The Wealth of Nations*, Smith argues that self-interest in the free market will naturally lead to the production of the correct amount of goods and services. Using a metaphor to support the idea of free trade, Smith claims that when people pursue what is in their own interest, there is a force also resulting in good consequences for others: "he intends only his own gain, and he is in this, as in many other cases, led by an invisible hand to promote an end which was not part of his intention." Smith believes that people will do what is in their own best interest but, nonetheless, "By pursuing his own interest he frequently promotes that of the society more effectually than when he really intends to promote it." In other words, Smith believes that when people act according to their own self-interest, it promotes the good of all. The idea advanced by modern economists, such as Friedman, of the invisible hand in the free market is that by allowing people to pursue self-interest in the form of profit, the best products will be produced, the best prices will be given to consumers, and any products needed by consumers will be produced—all of which results in the best outcome for all.

Economist Paul Krugman disagrees that reliance on the free market is always the best economic strategy, criticizing Friedman by contending, "he slipped all too easily into claiming both that markets always work and that only markets work."[2] Krugman, by contrast, believes that government intervention in the market is necessary. Economist Joseph E. Stiglitz does not agree with reliance on the invisible hand as a justification for the free market, arguing in his 2006 book *Making*

Globalization Work, "the reason that the invisible hand often seems invisible is that it is often not there."

One debate about capitalism is whether or not it is the best economic system. But among proponents of capitalism, a debate rages about the extent to which a capitalist economy should operate within a free market. America's current capitalistic economy does not exist in an entirely free market; for example, there are government regulations on labor, taxes on products and labor, and public ownership of certain services, including utilities. Among critics of the current system, some say that any problems in the system are caused by too much government intervention, while others contend that problems are caused by too little government intervention. This is just one of the ongoing debates about capitalism. By exploring some of these debates, including whether or not capitalism is a good economic system and whether government intervention in the capitalist system is ever warranted, *Current Controversies: Capitalism* helps to illuminate some of the most current debates about capitalism.

Notes

1. Milton Friedman, with the assistance of Rose D. Friedman, *Capitalism and Freedom.* Chicago: University of Chicago Press, 1962.
2. Paul Krugman, "Who Was Milton Friedman?" *The New York Review of Books,* vol. 54, no. 2, Feb. 15, 2007. www.nybooks. com/articles/19857.

CHAPTER 1

Is Capitalism a Good Economic System?

Overview: Capitalism

Jim Stanford

Jim Stanford is one of Canada's best-known economists. He works for the Canadian Auto Workers union and writes a regular economics column for the Globe and Mail.

In the early days of human civilization, the "economy" was a pretty simple affair. Our work consisted of hunting animals for meat, fur, and bones; gathering wild produce (like berries); and constructing simple shelters. These hunter-gatherer economies were often nomadic (moving in tune with the weather or animal migrations). They were cooperative, in that everyone in a family or clan grouping worked together (with some division of tasks across genders and ages). And they were mostly non-hierarchical: no-one "owned" anything or "hired" anyone. (While priests, chiefs, or other leaders had special authority, that authority did not derive from their economic position.) In general, these economies produced just enough to keep their members alive from one year to the next.

Surplus, Class, and Slavery

Eventually humans learned they could deliberately cultivate useful plants, and agriculture began. This caused corresponding social and economic changes. First, it allowed for permanent settlements (with the opportunity to build better homes and other structures). Second, the greater productivity of agriculture allowed society to generate an economic SURPLUS: production beyond what was required just to keep the producers alive. Third, with that surplus came the task of deciding how to use it. The existence of a surplus allowed some members of society, for the first time, not to work. This opened up a whole new can of worms. Who would avoid working on the farm? What would they do instead? And how would they keep the rest of society—those who had to continue working—in line?

With permanent settlements and a growing economic surplus, therefore, came the first CLASS divisions within society—in which different groups of people fulfilled fundamentally different economic roles, depending on their status and their relationship to work. Different economic systems handled this fundamental issue in different ways. For example, under monarchist systems, a powerful elite controlled the surplus and its allocation based on inherited birthright. The monarch needed the acceptance or at least acquiescence of his or her subjects, which generally needed to be imposed (from time to time, anyway) by brute force.

Many of these societies also relied on SLAVERY, where entire groups of people (often designated by race or caste) were simply forced to work, again through brute force. In case this sounds like ancient history, remember that the US economy (the most powerful capitalist country in the world) was based largely on slavery until fewer than 150 years ago, and human trafficking still forcibly enslaves millions of people around the world today. The resulting economic surplus was used in various ways: luxury consumption of the ruling elite; the construction of impressive buildings and monuments; the financing of exploration, war, and conquest; the work of non-agricultural artisans and scholars; and re-investment into new and improved economic techniques.

The existence of a surplus allowed some members of society, for the first time, not to work.

The Rise of Feudalism

While slavery and direct authoritarian rule were certainly powerful and straightforward ways for elites to control the economy and the resulting surplus, they had their drawbacks, too. Slaves and subjects often revolted. Their work ethic was not always the best: slaves tend to be grudging and bitter (for obvious reasons), requiring "active supervision" (often with a whip!) to elicit their effort and productivity.

Eventually a more subtle and ultimately more effective economic system evolved, called FEUDALISM. In this case, a more complex web of mutual obligations and rights was used to organize work and manage the surplus. Peasants were allowed to live on land that was governed by a higher class (gentry, landlords, or royalty). They could support themselves and their families, but in return had to transfer most of their surplus production to the gentry (in the form of annual payments or tithes). The gentry used this surplus to finance their own (luxury) consumption, the construction of castles, the work of artisans and priests, maintenance of a simple state apparatus, wars, and other "fringe" activities. In return, they were supposed to protect the peasantry on their land (from attack by competing landlords), and ensure their security.

Agriculture became steadily more productive (with the invention of techniques such as crop rotation, the use of livestock, and plant breeding). The surplus became larger, allowing the development of more complex and ambitious non-agricultural activities—including the emergence of a more powerful and well-resourced central government, more ambitious non-agricultural production (including the emergence of early manufacturing workshops), and farther-reaching exploration and conquest. More effective transportation (like ocean-going ships) allowed the development of long-range trade (bringing in specialty goods from far-flung colonies and trading partners). Later in the Middle Ages, this trade sparked the emergence of a whole new class: merchants, who earned an often-lucrative slice of the surplus by facilitating this growing trade. These merchants would play an important transitional role in the subsequent development of capitalism. . . .

The Evolution of Capitalism

The "birth" of capitalism, amidst the smoke and soot of the Industrial Revolution, was a painful and in many ways violent process. Workers were forced off their land and driven into cities, where they suffered horrendous exploitation and conditions that would be considered intolerable today: seven-day working weeks, twelve-hour working days, child labour, frequent injury, early death. Vast profits were earned by the new class of capitalists, most of which they ploughed back into new investment, technology, and growth—but some of which they used to finance their own luxurious consumption. The early capitalist societies were not at all democratic: the right to vote was limited to property owners, and basic rights to speak out and organize (including to organize unions) were routinely (and often violently) trampled.

The early capitalist societies were not at all democratic.

Needless to say, this state of affairs was not socially sustainable. Working people and others fought hard for better conditions, a fairer share of the incredible wealth they were producing, and democratic rights. Under this pressure, capitalism evolved, unevenly, toward a more balanced and democratic system. Labour laws established minimum standards; unions won higher wages; governments became more active in regulating the economy and providing public services. But this progress was not "natural" or inevitable; it reflected decades of social struggle and conflict. And progress could be reversed if and when circumstances changed—such as during times of war or recession. Indeed, the history of capitalism has been dominated by a rollercoaster pattern of boom, followed by bust.

The Golden Age of Capitalism

Perhaps the greatest bust of all, the Great Depression of the 1930s, spurred more changes. New banking regulations were aimed at preventing financial chaos. Government income-support and make-work projects tried to put people back to work. To some extent, these projects were influenced by the economic ideas of John Maynard Keynes. The greatest (and deadliest) make-work project was World War II. The war spurred massive military spending which suddenly kicked all the major economies back into high gear, and eliminated unemployment.

After World War II, a unique set of circumstances combined to create the most vibrant and in many ways most optimistic chapter in the history of capitalism—what is now often called the "Golden Age." This postwar boom lasted for about three decades, during which wages and living standards in the developed capitalist world more than doubled. Strong business investment (motivated in part by postwar recovery and rebuilding) was reinforced by a rapid expansion of government spending in most capitalist economies. Unemployment was low, productivity grew rapidly, yet profits (initially at least) were strong. This was also the era of the "Cold War" between capitalism (led by the US) and communism (led by the former Soviet Union). In this context, business leaders and Western governments felt all the more pressure to accept demands for greater equality and security, since they were forced by global geopolitics to defend the virtues of the capitalist system.

A More Aggressive Capitalism

It is now clear that beginning in the late 1970s, global capitalism entered a distinct and more aggressive phase. The previous willingness of business owners and governments to tolerate taxes, social programs, unions, and regulations petered out. Businesses and financial investors rebelled against shrinking profits, high inflation, militant workers, and international "instability" (represented most frighteningly by the success of left-wing revolutions in several countries in Asia, Africa, and

Latin America in the 1970s). They began to agitate for a new, harder-line approach—and eventually they got it.

Beginning in the late 1970s, global capitalism entered a distinct and more aggressive phase.

In retrospect, there were two clear "cannon shots" that signalled the beginning of this new chapter in the history of capitalism:

1. Paul Volcker became the head of the US Federal Reserve in 1979. He implemented very strict MONETARY POLICY, heavily influenced by the ideas of [American economist] Milton Friedman and the MONETARIST school [which posited a strong link between inflation and the money supply]. Interest rates rose dramatically, and economic growth slowed. Superficially, Volcker's high-interest-rate policy was motivated by a need to control and reduce inflation. But it quickly became clear that a deeper shift had occurred. Instead of promoting full employment as their top priority (as during the Golden Age), central bankers would now focus on strictly controlling inflation, protecting financial assets, and keeping labour markets strictly in check.

2. Margaret Thatcher was elected as UK [United Kingdom] Prime Minister in 1979, followed by the election of Ronald Reagan as US President a year later. Both advocated an aggressive new approach to managing the economy (and all of society) in the interests of private business. They fully endorsed the hard-line taken by Volcker (and his counterparts in other countries). They were even tougher in attacking unions and undermining labour law and social policies (Reagan crushed the US air traffic controllers' union in 1981, while Thatcher defeated the strong British miners' union in 1985). Reagan

and Thatcher shattered the broad Golden Age consensus, under which even conservative governments had accepted relatively generous social benefits and extensive government management of the economy. Despite forceful opposition in both countries, both leaders prevailed (supported by business interests), and became role models for hard-right conservatives in many other countries. Thatcher justified her initiatives with the now-classic (but false) slogan: "There is no alternative."

Neoliberalism

It gradually became clear that capitalism had fundamentally changed. The "kinder, gentler" improvements of the Golden Age era came under sustained attack, and would gradually (over the next quarter-century) be partially reversed—though not without a stubborn fightback by workers and communities. Some argued that capitalism could no longer afford those Golden Age programs; in my view, this is invalid, although there is no doubt that the Golden Age recipe began to encounter significant economic problems. Others argued that with the decline of communism and the weakening of left-wing parties, capitalism no longer *needed* to mollify its critics with compassionate policies (since it no longer faced a serious challenge to its continued existence).

This new era in capitalism has gone by several different names: neoconservativism, the "corporate agenda," and others. The most common term now used is NEOLIBERALISM. This term is confusing, since in some countries "liberal" refers to a centre or centre-left political ideology which still sees room for some Golden Age-style policies. In economics, however, "liberal" means something quite different: it means *an absence of government interference*. In this sense, "neoliberalism" implies going back to a more rough-and-tumble kind of capitalism, in which governments play a smaller role in regulating the economy and protecting social interests. But even this definition is not quite accurate: in fact, there are still many ways in which government and the state continue to wield real economic power under neoliberal capitalism. What has changed is *how*, and in *whose interests*, that power is now exercised.

Capitalism Is the Most Moral System

Craig Biddle

Craig Biddle is the editor and publisher of The Objective Standard, *a quarterly journal of culture and politics, and he is the author of* Loving Life: The Morality of Self-Interest and the Facts That Support It.

Capitalism enables everyone to act in a consistently self-interested manner. Rather than shying away from this unassailable fact, we must embrace and emphasize it. We must do so not on the pragmatic grounds that doing so will work to defend capitalism (which it will), but on the principled grounds that the selfishness-enabling characteristic of capitalism is, in fact, what makes it the only moral social system on earth.

To see why this is so, let us begin by observing how capitalism enables economic selfishness and what this means in practice.

Responsibility Under Capitalism

Under genuine capitalism—not the mongrel system operative in America today, but pure, unregulated, *laissez-faire* capitalism—the government prohibits citizens from using physical force against each other, and the Constitution prohibits the government from using force against citizens except in retaliation against those who initiate its use. Thus everyone is fully free to act on his own judgment for his own sake. . . .

If the bank employs rational policies and succeeds, its success is good for the bank, good for its owners, and good for its customers. If the bank engages in irrational policies—if, for instance, its risk-assessment procedures are such that it regularly lends money to people who cannot repay their loans—the bank suffers negative financial consequences. If its policies lead the bank to failure, it may not seek a bailout from the government; nor may the government offer to "rescue" the bank. Under capitalism, bankers and banks, like all individuals and businesses, are responsible for the consequences of their decisions, whether good or bad, profitable or not. Consequently, under capitalism, if a bank fails, it files bankruptcy or offers itself for sale on the cheap or goes out of business; its owners suffer losses; and its customers find other means through which to save or borrow money. Under capitalism, everyone is free to benefit from his rational choices and actions, and no one may force others to suffer the consequences of his irrational decisions.

Under capitalism, individuals and corporations legally own not only their profits but also their problems.

Capitalism and Rationality

Capitalism encourages rationality in the marketplace. Those who act in a rationally self-interested manner tend to succeed, and those who do succeed are free to enjoy the fruits of their rationality.

Consider the case of an automaker. Under capitalism, an automaker is free to manufacture and market cars in whatever way it sees fit, and the company is free to succeed or to fail accordingly. The government may not force the company to sell a particular kind of car, nor force it to pay its employees a particular minimum or maximum wage, nor force it to contract with a particular vendor, nor a union, nor anyone else. The automaker is free to make all such decisions according to its own judgment (i.e., the judgment of its owners). If the automaker uses good judgment and succeeds, it is free to keep, use, and dispose of its profits. If it uses poor judgment and fails—or if its competitors outperform it such that it cannot remain profitable—the automaker may file for bankruptcy or offer itself for sale or close its doors. But it may not seek a bailout from the government. Under capitalism, individuals and corporations legally own not only their profits but also their problems, and the government is prohibited from intervening in the marketplace.

As to unions, under capitalism, individuals are free to band together and to stipulate that members of their group will work only on certain terms and under certain conditions. But such groups may not force others to contract with them, nor may the government employ such force on their behalf. Under capitalism, everyone is free to set his own terms and conditions of contract; no one may infringe on the freedom of others to set theirs; everyone is equally free to be fully selfish.

Capitalism and Coercion

Capitalism is the system of mutual self-interest and mutual non-interference, everyone who wishes to live well and prosper is free to do so to the best of his effort and ability; no one may stop another from pursuing his values or goals.

Under capitalism, coercion is forbidden.

Consider a real-estate development company. Under capitalism, the company is free to build condominiums or pharmaceutical plants or whatever else it wants to build, and its owners are free to use and dispose of their profits according to their own judgment. But if the company needs to acquire real estate on which to build, it may acquire that property only from willing sellers. If, by mutual consent to mutual advantage, it can acquire the property from those who own it, the company is free to develop that property. If, however, the owners of the property in question do not want to sell it to the development the company may not force them to "sell"—nor may it enlist the government to do so. The company may increase its offer or change its plans or proceed peacefully in another manner, but it may not resort to coercion because, under capitalism, coercion is forbidden.

Capitalism and Freedom

Capitalism is the system of private property and voluntary exchange. Those who are willing to interact peacefully with others are free to produce, trade, and prosper accordingly. Those who wish to use force against their fellow men are precluded from doing so—and punished if they try.

Under capitalism, the initiation of physical force is barred from human relationships; citizens delegate the use of retaliatory force to the government, which may use force only in retaliation and only against those who initiate its use; and those who initiate force against others are met with force by the law. This arrangement leaves everyone free to act on his own judgment for his own sake as a matter of principle. This is what makes capitalism the system of selfishness—and this is what distinguishes capitalism from all other social systems.

Consider the alternative systems in this regard. Under *communism*, the government forces individuals and businesses to act against their judgment for the sake of the "workers" or the "community"; hence the term "communism" (e.g., the USSR [Union of Soviet Socialist Republics]). Under *socialism*, the government forces individuals and businesses to act against their judgment for the sake of the "collective" or "society"; hence the term "socialism" (e.g., present-day Sweden). Under *theocracy*, the government forces individuals and businesses to act against their judgment in obedience to "God's will"—or whatever His earthly "representatives" deem His will to be; hence the term "theocracy," which means literally "rule by God" (e.g., present-day Iran). Under *fascism*, the government forces individuals and businesses to act against their judgment for the sake of the "nation," the "race," the "people," the "eld-erly," the "poor," or some other "group"; hence the term "fas-cism," which means literally "group-ism" (e.g., Mussolini's Italy).

Under capitalism (which has yet to exist), the government is forbidden from forcing individuals or businesses to act against their judgment. In a capitalist society, everyone is le-gally free to act on his own judgment for his own sake. The government serves only to protect individuals and businesses from physical force by banning it from social relationships and by using retaliatory force as necessary against those who initiate its use. . . .

In a capitalist society, everyone is legally free to act on his own judgment for his own sake.

Individual Rights

Because an individual's judgment is his basic means of living, physical force, to the extent that it is used against him, causes him to lead a less than human life. This fact gives rise to man's need of a principle that precludes people, groups, and governments from using force against individuals. That prin-ciple is the principle of individual rights.

The principle of individual rights is the recognition of the fact that in order to live fully as a human being, an individual must be fully free to act on his own judgment for his own sake. If recognized and upheld, however, this principle would enable everyone to act consistently selfishly as a matter of principle—and this possibility runs counter to conventional morality.

This brings us to the crux of the battle for capitalism.

The Dominant Morality of Altruism

If human beings are to *act* on their rational judgment, they must be *free* to act on it. Capitalism is the social system that recognizes this fact and upholds the principle of individual rights. But according to the dominant morality today, altruism, the individual does not and cannot have a right to act on his own judgment for his own sake, because the individual has a "duty" to sacrifice his judgment and thus his life for the sake of others.

Whereas capitalism is the politics of self-interest and personal gain, altruism is the ethics of self-sacrifice and personal loss.

Altruism holds that being moral consists not in being selfish but in being self*less*, not in self-interestedly pursuing and protecting one's life-serving values but in self-sacrificially serving others. ("Alter" is Latin for "other"; "altruism" means "other-ism.") And because pushers of altruism frequently equivocate on the meaning of the concept of "service," it is crucial for advocates of capitalism to grasp the actual meaning of this concept as it relates to altruism.

Altruism does not call merely for "serving" others; it calls for *self-sacrificially* serving others. Otherwise, [American businessman and CEO of Dell, Inc.] Michael Dell would have to be considered more altruistic than Mother Teresa [a Catholic nun who devoted her life to serving the poor]. Why? Because Michael Dell serves millions more people than Mother Teresa ever did. The difference, of course, is in the way he serves people. Whereas Mother Teresa "served" people by exchanging her time and effort for *nothing*, Michael Dell serves people by *trading* with them—by exchanging value for value to mutual advantage—an exchange in which both sides *gain*.

Trading value for value is not the same thing as *giving up* values for nothing. There is a black-and-white difference between pursuing values and giving them up, between achieving values and relinquishing them, between exchanging a *lesser* value for a *greater* one and vice versa.

31

Sacrifice and Personal Loss

A sacrifice is not "any choice or action that precludes some other choice or action." A sacrifice is the surrender of a greater value for the sake of a lesser value or a non-value.

For example, if a parent forgoes a game of golf with his friend in order to spend the morning preparing for his son's birthday party that afternoon, he has not committed a sacrifice. If his son's party means more to his life than does the game of golf, then the sacrifice would be to forgo the preparation and play the game.

Similarly, if a student knows that his education is more important to his life than is a night on the town with his friends, then staying home to study for a crucial exam, against the urgings of his buddies, does not constitute a sacrifice. The sacrifice would be to forgo his judgment, hit the town, and botch the exam.

Likewise, if a man wants to become a banker because he is fascinated by the profession and thinks he will love that career, and if he forgoes his second choice, a career in law, in order to create a bank, then he has not committed a sacrifice. He has pursued the greater of the two values. If however, he decides to quit banking and become a bureaucrat on the grounds that selfless "public service" is the "right thing to do," then he has committed a sacrifice. He has abandoned what he regards as his ideal career in order to selflessly serve others— and, consequently, he will lead a less happy life.

Life requires that we regularly forgo lesser values for the sake of greater ones. But these are *gains*, not sacrifices. A sacrifice consists in giving up something that is *more* important to one's life for the sake of something that is *less* important (or non-important) to one's life. A sacrifice results in a *personal loss*.

Altruism and Self-Sacrifice

Whereas capitalism is the politics of self-interest and personal gain, altruism is the ethics of self-sacrifice and personal loss.

And altruism does not countenance self-interest or personal gain. This is not a caricature of altruism; it is the *essence* of the morality. As philosophy professor Peter Singer, an arch advocate of altruism, writes: "To the extent that [people] are motivated by the prospect of obtaining a reward or avoiding a punishment, they are not acting altruistically. . . ." As philosophy professor Thomas Nagel, another advocate of altruism, explains, altruism entails "a willingness to act in consideration of the interests of other persons, without the need of ulterior motives"—"ulterior motives" meaning: personal gains. And as the philosopher Ayn Rand, the arch opponent of altruism, succinctly put it: "The basic principle of altruism is that man has no right to exist for his own sake, that service to others is the only justification of his existence, and that self-sacrifice is his highest moral duty, virtue and value."

On the principle of altruism, a banker has no right to withhold a mortgage loan from someone on the selfish grounds that providing the loan would result in a loss; it is not moral to be "motivated by the prospect of obtaining a reward or avoiding a punishment"; it is wrong to selfishly pursue profit. He must serve others "without the need of ulterior motives"; he must *self-sacrificially* serve others—in this case, those who want to own a home.

Likewise, on the principle of altruism, an automaker has no right to pay employees an hourly rate that makes selfish sense for the business; it is wrong to establish terms and conditions with the "ulterior motive" of making money or remaining viable. The automaker must *self-sacrificially* serve others—such as union workers.

Nor on the principle of altruism does a property owner have a right to keep, use, and dispose of his belongings. If others—such as a real-estate development company whose proposed project would lead to higher tax revenues for the municipality—need the property owner's property, he has no right to withhold it for his selfish interests. According to altruism, he must "act in consideration of the interests of other persons"; he must *sacrifice* himself, his judgment, his property for the sake of others—in this case, the community-minded development company and the community it aims to "help."

No Reason to Sacrifice

Altruism, the morality that forbids people to act in a self-interested manner, is entirely incompatible with capitalism, the system that enables and encourages everyone to act in a *consistently* self-interested manner. Acceptance of the altruistic premise that being moral consists in self-sacrificially serving others is what gives rise to and supports the various forms of statism—communism, socialism, theocracy, fascism—and it is what is driving America toward tyranny today.

Human life requires capitalism: the social system of universal selfishness and prosperity.

The good news for lovers of liberty is that altruism is *false*. There are no facts that give rise to the notion that one should self-sacrificially serve others, which is why no one has ever presented such facts. Consequently, adherence to altruism is irrational. There is *no reason* to sacrifice, which is why no one has ever given a reason. As Ayn Rand pointed out:

> There is one word—a single word—which can blast the morality of altruism out of existence and which it cannot withstand—the word: "*Why?*" *Why* must man live for the sake of others? *Why* must he be a sacrificial animal? *Why* is that the good? There is no earthly reason for it—and, ladies and gentlemen, in the whole history of philosophy no *earthly* reason has ever been given.

Of course, alleged reasons have been given, but not legitimate ones. . . .

The Good of Self-Interest

There is no reason to sacrifice—but there *is* a reason to act in a self-interested manner: your life and happiness depend on it. And there is a reason to advocate a social system that enables you and everyone else to act in a self-interested manner: your life and happiness—and the lives and happiness of all your loved ones—depend on it. Reasons do not get any better than these.

Advocates of capitalism must come to see that self-sacrifice is not moral but evil—evil because it is irrational and anti-life. Man's life does not require that he give up the values on which his life depends. It requires the opposite. It requires that he pursue and protect his life-serving values. And it requires a social system that enables him to do so. Human life requires capitalism: the social system of universal selfishness and prosperity. And if we are to defend capitalism, we must repudiate the morality of self-sacrifice and embrace the morality of self-interest: rational egoism.

Rational egoism calls not for self-sacrifice but for rational self-interest (the only kind of self-interest there is). It calls for everyone to pursue his life-serving values while respecting the rights of others to do the same.

Egoism does not call for "doing whatever one pleases" or "doing whatever one feels like doing" or "stabbing others in the back to get what one wants." Those are caricatures of egoism perpetrated by pushers of altruism who seek to equate egoism with hedonism and subjectivism. Egoism does not hold pleasure or feelings as the standard of value. It holds *man's life* as the standard of value—and *reason* as man's basic means of living.

According to rational egoism, that which promotes man's life is good, and that which harms or destroys man's life is evil. There are several highly developed principles involved in this morality—including the supreme value of reason; the crucial need of purposeful goals and self-esteem; and the virtues of productiveness, independence, honesty, integrity, justice, and pride. But the key *political* principle of rational egoism is the principle of individual rights.

Egoism Supports Capitalism

Whereas egoism identifies the fact that people must think rationally and act accordingly in order to live and prosper, the principle of individual rights identifies the fact that if people are to act in accordance with their judgment, they must be *free* to do so. Whereas altruism underlies and supports statism, egoism underlies and supports capitalism.

As the politics of self-interest, capitalism cannot be defended with the ethics of self-sacrifice—nor can it be defended apart from a moral foundation (e.g., via libertarianism or mere economics). We who wish to advocate capitalism must advocate it explicitly on moral grounds. We must unabashedly explain to our allies and potential allies (i.e., people who are willing to think) that human life requires rationally self-interested action; that each individual has a moral right to act on his own judgment for his own sake, so long as he does not violate the same rights of others; that capitalism is moral because it enables everyone to act in a rationally self-interested manner; and that a mixed economy—in which no one's rights are fully protected, and everyone's rights are partially violated—is immoral because it precludes people from acting fully as human life requires.

We who wish to advocate capitalism must take the moral high ground—which is ours by logical right—and we must never cede an inch to those who claim that self-sacrifice is a virtue. It is not. Self-interest is a virtue. Indeed, acting in one's rational self-interest while respecting the rights of others to do the same is the *basic* requirement of human life. And capitalism is the only social system that fully legalizes it. Grounds do not get more moral than that.

The Free Market Has Promoted Virtues

Deirdre McCloskey

Deirdre McCloskey teaches economics, history, English, and communication at the University of Illinois at Chicago. She is the author of The Bourgeois Virtues: Ethics for an Age of Commerce.

I don't much care how "capitalism" is defined, so long as it is not defined a priori to mean vice incarnate. The prejudging definition was favored by [philosopher Jean-Jacques] Rousseau—though he did not literally use the word "capitalism," still to be coined—and by [French politician Pierre-Joseph] Proudhon, [German philosopher Karl] Marx, [Russian anarchist Mikhail] Bakunin, [Russian anarchist Peter] Kropotkin, [Polish revolutionary Rosa] Luxemburg, [sociologist Thorstein] Veblen, [anarchist Emma] Goldman, and [French philosopher Jean-Paul] Sartre. Less obviously, the same definition was used by their opponents [English philosopher Jeremy] Bentham, [English economist David] Ricardo, [Philosopher Ayn] Rand, [economist Milton] Friedman, and [economist Gary] Becker. All of them, left and right, have *defined* commercial society at the outset to be bad by any standard higher than successful greed.

Defining Capitalism

Such a definition makes pointless an inquiry into the good and bad of modern commercial society. If modern capitalism is defined to be *the same thing* as Greed—"the restless never-ending process of profit-making alone . . . , this boundless

Deirdre McCloskey, "Bourgeois Virtues?" *Cato Policy Report*, vol. 28, no. 3, May/June 2006, pp. 1, 8–11. Copyright © 2006 The Cato Institute. All rights reserved. Republished with permission of The Cato Institute, conveyed through Copyright Clearance Center, Inc. This article has been excerpted and edited for this publication.

greed after riches," as Marx put it in Chapter 1 of *Capital*, drawing on an anti-commercial theme originating in [Greek philosopher] Aristotle—then that settles it, before looking at the evidence.

There's no evidence, actually, that greed or miserliness or self-interest was new in the 16th or the 19th or any other century. "The infamous hunger for gold" is from *The Aeneid*, Book III, line 57, not from Benjamin Franklin or *Advertising Age*. The propensity to truck and barter is human nature. Commerce is not some evil product of recent manufacture. Commercial behavior is one of the world's oldest professions. We have documentation of it from the earliest cuneiform writing, in clay business letters from Kish or Ashur offering compliments to your lovely wife and making a deal for copper from Anatolia or lapis lazuli from Afghanistan. Bad and good behavior in buying low and selling high can be found anywhere, any time.

Commerce is not some evil product of recent manufacture.

To put the matter positively, we have been and can be virtuous and commercial, liberal and capitalist, democratic and rich. As John Mueller said in *Capitalism, Democracy, and Ralph's Pretty Good Grocery*, "Democracy and capitalism, it seems, are similar in that they can often work pretty well even if people generally do not appreciate their workings very well."

One of the ways capitalism works "pretty well," Mueller and I and a few other loony pro-capitalists such as Michael Novak and James Q. Wilson and Hernando De Soto and the late Robert Nozick claim, is to nourish the virtues. Mueller argues for one direction of causation: "Virtue is, on balance and all other things being equal, essentially smart business under capitalism: nice guys, in fact, tend to finish first." Max Weber had a century earlier written to the same effect: "Along with clarity of vision and ability to act, it is only by virtue [note the word] of very definite and highly developed ethical qualities that it has been possible for [an entrepreneur of this new type] to command the indispensable confidence of his customers and workmen."

The Benefits of Growth

The material side of capitalist and bourgeois success is, of course, wonderful. "Modern economic growth," as the economists boringly call the fact of real income per person growing at a "mere" 1.5 percent per year for 200 years, to achieve a rise in per capita income by a factor of 19 in the countries that most enthusiastically embraced capitalism, is certainly the largest change in the human condition since the ninth millennium BC. It ranks with the first domestications of plants and animals and the building of the first towns. Possibly, modern economic growth is as large and important an event in human history as the sudden perfection of language, in Africa around 80,000 to 50,000 BC. In a mere 200 years our bourgeois capitalism has domesticated the world and made it, from Chicago to Shanghai, into a single, throbbing city.

The material side of capitalist and bourgeois success is, of course, wonderful.

I honor the material success and start every class I give on history or economics by showing an imagined chart extending from one side of the room to the other in which income per head bounces along at $1 a day for 80,000 to 50,000 years . . . and then in the last 200 years explodes, to the $109 a day the average American now earns. Your ancestors and mine were dirt-poor slaves, and ignorant. We should all make sure that people grasp that capitalism and freedom, not government "programs," have made us rich.

The Effects of Enrichment

But we should emphasize, too, as Benjamin Friedman does in his recent book, *The Moral Consequences of Economic Growth*, the ethical and political effects of enrichment. The combination of longer and richer lives since 1800 is one reason that liberty has spread. There are by now many more adults living long enough lives sufficiently free from desperation to have some political interests. The theory that economic desperation leads to good revolution is, of course, mistaken, or else our freedoms would have emerged from the serfs of Russia or the peasants of China, not from the bourgeoisie of northwestern Europe, as they did in fact. Material wealth can yield political or artistic wealth. It doesn't have to, but it can. And it often has. What emerged from Russia and China, remember, were the anti-bourgeois nightmares of [Joseph] Stalin and Mao [Zedong].

And the enrichment in "expected adult years of goods-supplied life" has cultural effects, too, very big ones, as Tyler Cowen has taught us in his books, such as *In Praise of Commercial Culture*. The factor of increase since great-great-great-great grandma's day is about 42.5. The longer, richer average now applies to six billion rather than to the former one billion people. So multiply each by a factor of six to get the increase in "world adult materially supplied years." The result is a factor of 255. It nurtured the flowers of world culture, low and high, politics and music.

[Ludwig van] Beethoven, for example, in a world sized about 1.0 in such terms, was among the first highbrow musicians to support himself by selling his compositions to the public rather than to a noble patron. A market of bourgeois minipatrons was just emerging. [Joseph] Haydn had shown what could be done for musical art on the frontier of capital-. ism, moving in 1791 from the livery of Prince Miklós Esterházy of Hungary to popular acclaim and commercial success as a bourgeois composer in London. That's 255 times more music, painting, and the rest, good and bad, glorious and corrupting. As a couple of acute observers, Marx and [Friedrich] Engels, put it when all this was getting under way, "What earlier century had even a presentiment that such productive forces slumbered in the lap of social labor?"

Capitalism and the bourgeois life can be, and to some extent already are, virtuous.

Ethics for a World of Commerce

Nonetheless, it is still routine to idealize a pagan or a Christian story of the virtues and then to sound a lament that in these latter days, alas, no one achieves the ideal. We live in a vulgar age of iron, or of plastic, it is said, not pagan gold or Christian silver. In the ethical accounting of artists and intellectuals since 1848, the townsfolk are perhaps useful, even necessary; but *virtuous?* The aristocracy and peasantry-proletariat, it is reported by the clerisy, join in disdain for the merchant, who has neither the martial honor of a knight nor the solidarity of a serf. The bourgeois virtues have been reduced to the single vice of greed.

It's not so. Capitalism and the bourgeois life can be, and to some extent already are, virtuous. That is, bourgeois life *improves us ethically*, and would have even if it had not also made us rich. I realize that such optimism is not widely credited. It makes the clerisy uneasy to be told that they are *better* people for having the scope of a modern and bourgeois life. They quite understandably want to honor their poor ancestors in the Italy of old or their poor cousins in India now, and feel impelled to claim with anguish as they sip their caramel macchiato grandes that their prosperity comes at a *terrible* ethical cost.

On the political left it has been commonplace for the past century and a half to charge that modern, industrial people are alienated, rootless, angst ridden, superficial, materialistic, and that it is precisely participation in markets that has made them so. Gradually the right and the middle have come to accept the charge. Some sociologists, both progressive and conservative, embrace it, lamenting the decline of organic solidarity. By the early 21st century, some on the right have schooled themselves to reply to the charge with a sneering cynicism, "Yeah, sure. Markets have no morals. So what? Greed is good. Bring on the pizza."

But it's not so.

A little farmers' market opens before 6:00 a.m. on a summer Saturday at Polk and Dearborn in Chicago. As a woman walking her dog passes the earliest dealer setting up his stall, the woman and the dealer exchange pleasantries about the early bird and the worm. The two people here are enacting a script of citizenly courtesies and of encouragement for prudence and enterprise and good relations between seller and buyer. Some hours later the woman is moved to buy $1.50 worth of tomatoes from him. But that's not the point. The market was an occasion for virtue, an expression of solidarity across gender, social class, ethnicity.

Markets and the bourgeois life are not always bad for the human spirit.

The Seven Virtues

In other words, markets and the bourgeois life are not always bad for the human spirit. In certain ways, and on balance, they have been good.

How so? The virtues came to be gathered by the Greeks, the Romans, the Stoics, the Church, [Scottish economist] Adam Smith, and recent "virtue ethicists" into a coherent ethical framework. Until the framework somewhat mysteriously fell out of favor among theorists in the late 18th century, most

Westerners did not think in Platonic terms of the One Good—to be summarized, say, as Maximum Utility, or as the Categorical Imperative, or as the Idea of the Good. They thought in Aristotelian terms of Many Virtues, plural.

"We shall better understand the nature of the ethical character," said Aristotle, "if we examine its qualities one by one." That still seems a sensible plan. Since about 1958 in English a so-called virtue ethics—as distinct from the Kantian, Benthamite, or contractarian views that dominated ethical philosophy from the late 18th century until then—has revived Aristotle's one-by-one program. "We might," wrote Iris Murdoch in 1969, early in the revival, "set out from an ordinary language situation by reflecting upon the virtues . . . since they help to make certain potentially nebulous areas of experience more open to inspection." That again seems reasonable. Here are the Western Seven with exemplars.

- Faith—St. Peter

- Hope—Martin Luther King Jr.

- Love—Emma Goldman

- Justice—Gandhi

- Courage—Achilles, Shane

- Temperance—Socrates, Jane Austin

- Prudence—Ben Franklin

The system is a jury-rigged combination of the "pagan" virtues appropriate to a free male citizen of Athens (Courage, Temperance, Justice, and Prudence) and the "Christian" virtues appropriate to a believer (Faith, Hope, and Love).

Jury-rigged or not, the Seven cover what we need in order to flourish as human beings. So also might other ethical systems—Confucianism, for example, or Talmudic Judaism, or Native American shamanism—and these can be lined up beside the Seven for comparison. There are many ways to be human. But it is natural to start with the Seven, since they are the ethical tradition of a West in which bourgeois life first came to dominance.

The Bourgeois Virtues

What then *are* the bourgeois virtues?

The leading bourgeois virtue is the Prudence to buy low and sell high. I admit it. There. But it is also the prudence to trade rather than to invade, to calculate the consequences, to pursue the good with competence—[President] Herbert Hoover, for example, energetically rescuing many Europeans from starvation after 1918.

Another bourgeois virtue is the Temperance to save and accumulate, of course. But it is also the temperance to educate oneself in business and in life, to listen to the customer, to resist the temptations to cheat, to ask quietly whether there might be a compromise here—Eleanor Roosevelt negotiating the United Nations Declaration of Human Rights in 1948.

A third is the Justice to insist on private property honestly acquired. But it is also the justice to pay willingly for good work, to honor labor, to break down privilege, to value people for what they can do rather than for who they are, to view success without envy, making capitalism work since 1776.

A fourth is the Courage to venture on new ways of business. But it is also the courage to overcome the fear of change, to bear defeat unto bankruptcy, to be courteous to new ideas, to wake up the next morning and face fresh work with cheer, resisting the despairing pessimism of the clerisy from 1848 to the present. And so the bourgeoisie can have Prudence, Temperance, Justice, and Courage, the pagan four. Or the Scottish three—Prudence, Temperance, and Justice, the artificial virtues—plus enterprise, that is, Courage with another dose of Temperance.

Beyond Pagan Virtues

Beyond the pagan virtues is the Love to take care of one's own, yes. But it is also a bourgeois love to care for employees and partners and colleagues and customers and fellow citizens, to wish all of humankind well, to seek God, finding human and transcendent connection in the marketplace in 2006, and in a Scottish benevolence c. 1759.

Another is the Faith to honor one's community of business. But it is also the faith to build monuments to the glorious past, to sustain traditions of commerce, of learning, of religion, finding identity in Amsterdam and Chicago and Osaka.

Another is the Hope to imagine a better machine. But it is also the hope to see the future as something other than stagnation or eternal recurrence, to infuse the day's work with a purpose, seeing one's labor as a glorious calling, 1533 to the present. So the bourgeoisie can have Faith, Hope, and Love, these three, the theological virtues.

The bourgeois virtues are merely the Seven Virtues exercised in a commercial society. They are not hypothetical. For centuries in Venice and Holland and then in England and Scotland and British North America, then in Belgium, Northern France, the Rhineland, Sydney, Cleveland, Los Angeles, Bombay, Shanghai, and in a widening array of places elsewhere, against hardy traditions of aristocratic and peasant virtues, we have practiced them. We have fallen repeatedly, of course, into bourgeois vices. Sin is original. But we live in a commercial society, most of us, and capitalism is not automatically vicious or sinful. Rather the contrary.

"Bourgeois virtues," is no contradiction. It is the way we live now, mainly, at work, on our good days, and the way we should, Mondays through Fridays.

Reclaiming "Bourgeois"

I would like to recover the word "bourgeois," taking it back from its enemies. The word "capitalist," referring in the opinion of Communists in the 1880s to greedy monopolists of the means of production, was taken back in the 1980s to mean "advocates for and actors in free markets." "Quaker" and "Tory" originated as sneers but were calmly appropriated by the victims and made honorable.

In April 1566, 200 armed and Protestant-sympathizing aristocrats from the Low Countries presented a petition to Margaret of Parma, Catholic Philip's regent in Brussels, urging her to grant religious tolerance. She was advised by one of her counselors to pay them no heed. They were merely, said he in his aristocratic French, "*gueux*," that is, "beggars." Never mind that the petitioners were themselves French-speaking aristocrats.

The noblemen seized upon the word, and called themselves proudly thereafter Beggars, Dutch *Geuzen*. Baron Henry Brederode, their leader, was called *Le Grand Gueux*. That summer the new word was claimed too by the Protestant iconoclasts. "*Vivent les Gueux*," the rioters cried in Antwerp.

The word has remained alive in the Dutch language. The pirate navy that took Brill from the Spanish in 1572 called itself the *Watergeuzen*, Sea Beggars. The orthodox Calvinists marching to kill off toleration in 1616 called themselves the Mud Beggars. One of the illegal newspapers during the German occupation of World War II was *De Geus*, The Beggar. The normal Dutch word for such reversals of a sneer became *geuzennamen*, beggars-names.

I hope to make "bourgeois" a *geuzennaam*, to remake a word of contempt into a word of honor.

Capitalism Is Practical and Moral

Robert W. Tracinski

Robert W. Tracinski is editor of the Intellectual Activist, *a monthly magazine, and* TIADaily.com, *which offers daily news and analysis from a pro-reason, pro-individualist perspective.*

The worldwide discrediting of socialism has left our intellectual leaders in an odd dilemma. The system that they hailed for decades as a moral and philosophical ideal has been shown to be disastrous in practice, leading to stagnation at best and starvation at worst. Meanwhile, capitalism has led to the creation of unprecedented wealth, advanced technology, and widespread prosperity. Yet capitalism is denounced by these same intellectuals as a system of greed, materialism, and ruthless "dog-eat-dog" competition.

An Apparent Contradiction

So it would seem that the system that enforces virtue leads to poverty—while the system that encourages vice leads to prosperity.

There must be a trade-off, in this view, between being moral and being practical. Given this alternative, the cynical "realists" choose the practical. They conclude that some degree of vice must be tolerated in order to achieve the higher "social good" of prosperity, so they seek a "third way" compromise between the moral ideal of socialism and the practical necessity of capitalism. But the "idealists" will have none of this, so they conclude that if capitalism leads to prosperity, then prosperity itself must be evil. They declare that affluence is a disease and join the environmentalists.

But there is another answer to this dilemma; there is a solution to this apparent contradiction between the moral and the practical. That solution is to re-examine the premise that capitalism is immoral. If we do this, we can see that every characteristic that makes capitalism practical is also a principle that makes capitalism moral.

Every characteristic that makes capitalism practical is also a principle that makes capitalism moral.

The Practical Nature of Capitalism

Capitalism is practical, many economists have argued, because it allows individuals to act on their own thinking rather than being forced to obey the decrees of bureaucrats. Under capitalism, every problem of economic production is tackled by thousands, even millions, of minds. The people whose thinking is successful will thrive. They succeed because they find opportunities that others don't see, because they develop new products that no one else has thought of, or because they discover more efficient production methods that have never been tried before.

In a free market, where everyone is free to start a business, raise capital, and place his product on the market—each individual thinker has the opportunity to put his ideas into practice, and to succeed or fail based on the merits of his idea. Those who succeed bring us new and improved products at an ever lower cost, creating economic progress and prosperity.

In the regulatory state, by contrast, the edicts of politicians and bureaucrats override the thinking of individuals. The result is that political expediency, rather than the truth or falsity of an idea, determines who gets to put his ideas into practice. Thus, for example, a popular health scare about silicone implants or electric power lines is backed by judicial action, in defiance of provable scientific facts; the congressional districts in which ethanol is produced are regarded as more important than the fuel's economic value; a union leader's ability to deliver votes trumps the employer's judgment concerning what he can afford to pay; and so on.

Stated in more fundamental terms, it is the rational thinking of individuals that causes the production of wealth. But government regulation acts to stymie individual thought, subordinating the knowledge and creativity of millions of individuals to the edicts of public officials.

Thus, the practical value of capitalism flows from the need to protect the creativity and freedom of thought of the individual. But isn't this also a profound *moral* principle? Most of today's intellectuals still recognize that we need to protect the thinking of the artist or the scientist—but the same principle applies equally to the worker, the executive, and the industrialist. Only capitalism fully recognizes the moral right of the individual to think and to act on his thinking—not just in his personal life or intellectual life, but also in his economic life.

The Rewards of Capitalism

Economic production is not just a matter of thinking; it is also a matter of motivation. Thus, according to economists, the practicality of capitalism also stems from the fact that it allows individuals to set their own plans and pursue their own goals. Individuals are allowed to decide what career they would enjoy most; what products would give them the best value for their money; what opportunities would give them the best return on their investment; and so on. And capitalism does not merely offer the individual the freedom to pursue his own goals; it also rewards him for doing so. It offers him, as an incentive and reward for achieving his ambitions, the prospect of making money. As a result, people in a free market will work harder, longer, and smarter; they will take more risks and endure more hardships—so long as the work is theirs to choose and theirs to profit from.

In a state-run economy, by contrast, the central planning of government officials wipes out the plans of individuals. Since they don't own the business, can't control the course of their own careers, and don't stand to gain or lose from their actions, the workers' predominant attitude is apathy. And why should they care? If they succeed in increasing production, the extra wealth will be used to support those who haven't succeeded. "From each according to his ability, to each according to his need" is the motto of the welfare state. But in such a system, who would want to be the man of ability, conscripted into a life of unrewarded drudgery so that others can consume the product of his labor? It is no surprise that every society that has approached this socialist ideal has found few volunteers to be the men of ability who keep the economy running.

The fundamental characteristics that make capitalism practical—its respect for the freedom of the mind and for the sanctity of the individual—are also profound moral ideals.

Stated in more fundamental terms, capitalism is practical because it relies on the inexhaustible motive-power of self-interest. Under capitalism, people are driven by loyalty to their own goals and by the ambition to improve their lives. They are driven by the idea that one's own life is an irreplaceable value not to be sacrificed or wasted.

But this is also a crucial moral principle: the principle that each man is an end in himself, not a mere cog in the collective machine to be exploited for the ends of others. Most of today's intellectuals reflexively condemn self-interest; yet this is the same quality enshrined by our nation's founders when they proclaimed the individual's right to "the pursuit of happiness." It is only capitalism that recognizes this right.

The fundamental characteristics that make capitalism practical—its respect for the freedom of the mind and for the sanctity of the individual—are also profound moral ideals. This is the answer to the dilemma of the moral vs. the practical. The answer is that capitalism is a system of *virtue*—the virtues of rational thought, productive work, and pride in the value of one's own person. The reward for these virtues—and for the political system that protects and encourages them—is an ever-increasing wealth and prosperity.

The Capitalist Wage System Entails Exploitation

Rick Wolff

Rick Wolff is professor of economics at University of Massachusetts–Amherst, and he helped to launch Rethinking Marxism, *a journal of economics, culture, and society.*

When [German philosopher Karl] Marx referred to workers in capitalism as "wage-slaves" he meant more than a striking phrase. For him, the analogy between slavery and capitalism offered a powerful contribution to anti-capitalist movements. The clue to that contribution lies in the *Communist Manifesto's* summary of what differentiated communists from other leftists: the latter seek to raise wages, the former to abolish the wage system.

Opposition to Slavery

While slavery emerged at different times and places in world history, it always generated opponents. Among the enslaved and others, two kinds of opposition arose. The first focused on improving the slaves' living conditions: these opponents demanded that slaves be better fed, clothed, housed, treated, and so on. The second made a very different demand: slavery as an institution had to be abolished. The two oppositions sometimes collaborated, but they sometimes fought each other bitterly. Then the first accused the second of an irresponsible utopianism that sacrificed action for the immediate improvement of slaves' lives and aimed instead for what at best was a distant goal. The second retorted that so long as slavery survived as an institution, improvements for slaves would be difficult to achieve, insufficient, and insecure; moreover, by limiting the opposition's goal to improving slaves' conditions, slavery as an institution was condoned and the movement for abolition weakened.

Although slavery lasted for long periods in many places, eventually the second sort of opposition prevailed. Across much of the modern "civilized" world, slavery was abolished as an intrinsically immoral and inhumane institution regardless of whether the slaves' enjoyed good conditions or not. The fourteenth amendment to the US Constitution outlawed the institution of slavery for all except prison inmates. Predictably, the de-facto slavery of prison inmates has everywhere generated, once again, the same two sorts of oppositions.

For Marx, the crux of the issue is that capitalism entails exploitation.

Marx's Opposition to Capitalism

When Marx likened wage-workers to slaves, he brought the lessons of oppositions to slavery to the emerging movements against capitalism. Put bluntly, Marx argued against forms of anti-capitalism that limited themselves to improving workers' living conditions. Fast-forwarding to today, Marx would criticize movements such as those for "a living wage" or "pension reform" or "welfare increases" or "saving social security" and so on. A Marxist opposition to capitalism is rather one focused on its abolition as a system. Marxists, he might say, are to capitalism what abolitionists were to slavery.

For Marx, the crux of the issue is that capitalism entails *exploitation*. A large part of the population (productive laborers) produces a surplus that is appropriated and distributed by a small part of the population (capitalists). In capitalist enterprises, workers are hired only if the value that their labor adds (to the raw materials, tools, and equipment their work uses up) exceeds the value paid to them as wages for doing that labor. That excess value—the surplus—belongs to the capitalists since they own the outputs of production, sell them in markets, and thereby realize the surplus value in them. In the preferred language of capitalism, that surplus value comprises the "profits" of the capitalists, their "private property" to dispense in their own interests.

The less wages that capitalists must pay to workers, the more surplus they get for themselves. Exploitation thus situates tension, hostility, and conflict in the heart of production. Capitalists and workers are set into oppositional struggles. Moreover, those struggles ramify and provoke competitive struggles among capitalists and among workers. Alongside the outputs of capitalist production yielding impressive incomes and accumulating wealth, there are also the countless, ramifying social costs of the conflicts and competitions.

By excluding them from the surplus, exploitation also excludes workers from the tasks, skills, and rewards of organizing, managing, and directing production. Workers and capitalists thus become systemically unequal in ability, competence, and confidence. The inequalities anchored in capitalist production usually carry over to make the politics and cultures of capitalist societies similarly unequal. The absence of democracy in production undermines efforts to establish it in politics.

Neoclassical Economic Theory

Capitalist exploitation would be difficult to sustain if it had to be imposed on workers resentful of their exploitation and its social effects. Hence, as with all other exploitative systems (e.g., feudalism and slavery), theories are advanced and disseminated by capitalism's organic intellectuals that make exploitation invisible and so function to deny its existence. Such theories parallel their counterparts in slavery and feudalism where it was argued that slaves and serfs were not exploited but were rather protected (saved from despair, poverty, and death), loved like children, culturally uplifted, and so on by their lords and masters.

Today, the hegemonic [the predominant influence of one group over another or others] economic theory, called "neoclassical economics" for historical reasons, serves to make exploitation invisible. Building on the early formulation of such ideas by Adam Smith [a Scottish moral philosopher and a pioneer of political economy], neoclassical economics casts production as a process in which no surplus gets produced, nor appropriated, nor distributed. Instead, production is an harmonious collaboration: workers bring their labor, landlords their land, and capitalists their capital. All three contribute to production and all three share in its fruits according to their contributions: the workers' share is wages, the landlords' is rent, and the capitalists' is profit. It is a world of fairness and harmony. The inability of workers to contribute capital is explained by their failure to save out of their incomes and their resulting lack of capital to contribute to production. The capital in the hands of capitalists is not the fruit of exploitation, of taking a surplus from workers, but rather the fruit of their own virtuous frugality. Capitalism fairly rewards individuals for the contributions each brings to production. More than that, capitalism represents an engine of wealth production, economic growth, and thus the possibility for everyone to become rich. Those who have failed to do so should chiefly blame themselves. To blame capitalism is not a valid social critique but rather the whining of losers.

Capitalist exploitation would be difficult to sustain if it had to be imposed on workers resentful of their exploitation and its social effects.

The Wage Concept

Neoclassical economic theory, among other hegemonic sets of ideas, has worked well to support and justify capitalism and undermine the appeal of Marxist economic theory. One modality of its working has been the sedimentation into the popular consciousness of the notion of "the wage." It strikes vast numbers of people as somehow obvious, natural, and necessary that production be organized around a deal struck between a wage payer and wage receiver. And this is all the more remarkable in as much as the vast bulk of human history displays economic systems without wages (neither serfs, nor slaves, nor individuals who work alone, nor most collective work systems have used wages). Capitalism's history is in part the history of the deepening conceptual hegemony of the wage. Thus, for example, the individual peasant or craftsperson working alone has had to be renamed a "self-employed person" to revision a non-wage production system as if it were waged.

Naturalizing the wage concept works to naturalize capitalist relations of production, the employer/employee relation, not as one among alternative production systems but as somehow intrinsic to production itself. Workers, trade unions, and intellectuals often cannot imagine production without wages and hence wage payers juxtaposed to wage earners. This helps to make capitalism itself appear as necessary and eternal much as the parallel theories celebrating feudalism and slavery performed the same function for those systems of production. The naturalization of the wage system helps support the notion that the fundamental goal of workers' organization must be to raise wages.

Thus, no surprise attaches to the fact, these days, that one widespread kind of social criticism concentrates on softening capitalism's negative impacts on workers and the larger society. It seeks to raise workers' wages and benefits and to make governments limit capitalists' rapaciousness and the social costs of their competition. In the US, this is what "liberals" do: from the minimalist oppositions within the Democratic Party to the demands of social democrats and many "radicals" for major wage increases, major government interventions, and so on. What always frustrates liberals and radicals is the difficulty of achieving these improved workers' conditions and the insecurity and temporariness of whatever improvements they do achieve. Today they bemoan yet another roll-back of improvements, namely those won under FDR's [President Franklin Delano Roosevelt] New Deal, [President John F.] Kennedy's New Frontier, and so on.

Marxists find capitalist exploitation to be as immoral and inhumane as slavery.

A Marxist Program

Marxism is that other kind of opposition that demands the abolition of capitalism as a system. Since Marxists find capitalist exploitation to be as immoral and inhumane as slavery, they might logically seek a further amendment to the US Constitution that abolishes it as well. A Marxist program would seek to replace capitalist production by a non-wage system, one where the workers will not only produce surpluses but also be their own boards of directors. The "associated workers" would, as Marx suggested, appropriate their own surpluses and distribute them. The wage-payer versus wage-recipient division of people inside production would vanish. Every worker's job description would entail not only his/her technical responsibilities to produce a specific output but also her/his responsibilities as part of the collective that appropriates and distributes the surplus. Monday to Thursday, each worker in each enterprise makes commodities, and every Friday, each worker functions as a member of that enterprise's board of directors. The stakes here are less [about] obtaining higher wages than [about] abolishing the wage system.

The point of such a Marxist program is to overcome the conflicts, wastes, and inequalities (economic, political, and cultural) that flow from the existence of capitalist exploitation whether or not wages are raised. The point is likewise to stress the incompatibility of any genuine democracy with the wage system and its usual social effects (and again whether wages are higher or lower).

Abolishing Exploitation

Of course, in the struggle between such a Marxist perspective and its various critics, the latter will depict the programmatic advocacy of an end to the wage system as impracticable, utopian, or deluded. Those persuaded by neoclassical economics will simply dismiss or ignore not only the Marxist criticism of the wage system but Marxism altogether. For them, the wage system is not only eternal and necessary, but also fair and "efficient." For them, since there "is" no surplus, they need not read or learn Marxist theory and criticism, let alone debate it. So Marxist theory and its proponents can be and are largely excluded from public discourse in the media, the schools, and politics.

For liberals suspicious of neoclassical economics—or "neoliberalism" as it is now more often called—the Marxian program sketched above would be seen as utopian fantasy at best. Yet, not the least irony of [President George W.] Bush's America today is how his regime's relentless removal or reduction of the past reforms (high wages, pensions, medical insurance, social security, state social programs, etc.) makes a liberal politics today seem painfully deluded to so many. The liberals seem hopelessly weak, unable to stop let alone reverse the Bush juggernaut. Worse still, what they advocate are precisely the reforms now being dismantled and thus revealed as having been fundamentally insecure all along. The audience for capitalism's critics and opponents is thus being primed to listen rather attentively to Marxist claims that an abolition of the wage system offers not only a better society but also a far better basis for *securing* those improvements in wages and working conditions that mass action can achieve. What is needed now are Marxists able and willing to articulate those claims to that audience, to persuade ever more of capitalism's critics and opponents that abolition of exploitation and the wage system must be a component of their program for social change.

The Values of Neoliberal Capitalism Have Had Terrible Consequences

Michael Leon Guerrero

Michael Leon Guerrero is co-coordinator of the Grassroots Global Justice Alliance, an organization that works to build power for working and poor people.

In the U.S., far-Right Republicans and Democratic liberals alike have sold many people on the notion that the market should be the main force to drive the economy and define social relationships. They maintain that government should stay off of peoples' backs and out of our wallets. They promote rugged individualism and consumerism couched in terms like "personal responsibility," "freedom" and "independence." "Greed is good!" was the mantra of Michael Douglas' character, Gordon Gecko, in the 1980s movie *Wall Street*, and those became the words to live by in the [19]80's and 90's. The philosophy and value of greed was taken to heart by many a corporate CEO, and, over the past 3 decades, this twisted logic—underlined by the values of individualism and the culture of consumerism—has turned back the clock on human development with devastating consequences.

The Chicago Boys' Disaster

Naomi Klein's landmark work *The Shock Doctrine: The Rise of Disaster Capitalism* summarizes the last thirty years of the neoliberal (aka [also known as] neoconservative) project. These policies have had a stranglehold on the global economy for decades. But Klein argues persuasively that it is primarily

Michael Leon Guerrero, "From the Ashes of Neoliberalism," This article was originally commissioned by the Center for Community Change for the Convening on Community Values, May 19–20, 2008. Reproduced by permission of the author.

in moments of societal or natural upheaval that capitalist extremists, trained by gurus like Milton Friedman at the University of Chicago, have been most able to impose their political and economic agenda. Even if a natural disaster didn't present itself, Friedman's disciples, like [Henry] Kissinger, [Richard] Nixon, [Ronald] Reagan, [George H. W.] Bush and [Bill] Clinton, had no problem wreaking their own violent havoc on vulnerable countries.

By now, the mantra of the "Chicago Boys" has become all too familiar: eliminate regulations, cut taxes, slash public spending, privatize public services, etc. Their policies dominated the global political landscape, unraveling the gains of centuries of social movements, while a new global elite has been enriched beyond imagination. A handful of people have become super-wealthy, and mega corporations have become even bigger and more powerful.

A handful of people have become super-wealthy, and mega corporations have become even bigger and more powerful.

Capitalism Unchecked

"Free trade" policies and the loan sharks that have run the World Bank and the International Monetary Fund have destroyed national economies. Millions of people have been forced into poverty, and entire communities have been displaced from the countryside. Multi-nationals and northern industrial nations siphon wealth from the developing countries. Those that migrate from their homelands to make a living in the north are greeted with walls, bullets and racism. In the U.S., millions are homeless, unemployed, in prison, or one paycheck away from bankruptcy. The social wage has been beaten down to unsustainable levels—real wages are lower now than they were 30 years ago. Yet the costs of fuel and raw materials have skyrocketed causing worldwide food shortages.

We have wiped out public budgets by eliminating taxes on those who profit most. Vital public infrastructure and services cannot meet basic needs like maintaining the levees in New Orleans and reconstructing the Gulf Coast [after the damage caused by Hurricane Katrina in 2005], or controlling the devastating blazes in Southern California. Yet the majority of our federal budget sponsors the wars and occupation in the Middle East, the warehousing of generations of the poor and people of color, the witch-hunt of immigrant refugees of U.S. foreign and trade policy, and the growing national debt.

Capitalism unchecked has given us Big Oil, Blood Diamonds, Enron and Halliburton. They have given us Afghanistan, Iraq, Guantanamo and the Wall of Death on the U.S.-Mexico border.

A Declining Empire

The rise of the neoliberal regime has occurred in the same era that we are experiencing the decline of the economic and political dominance of the United States empire. Scholar Immanuel Wallerstein observes that economically the U.S. has been losing its top economic position since the 1970s as other regional economies have expanded. The U.S. is staring economic collapse in the face, driven by the bursting of the housing bubble. This bust is enough to make even billionaire George Soros nervous, arguing that there is a profound difference between this downturn and other recent ones:

> "... the current crisis marks the end of an era of credit expansion based on the dollar as the international reserve currency. The periodic crises were part of a larger boom-bust process. The current crisis is the culmination of a super-boom that has lasted for more than 60 years."

Soros argues that with the deregulation of the financial industry, many of the mechanisms put in place to withstand a significant bust cycle have been eliminated. The Federal Reserve and the government may no longer have the tools to stave off a recession.

Today, the United States is the leader in a number of shameful statistics: the highest percentage and total numbers of its population in prison, the highest consumption of the world's natural resources, the only industrialized nation without universal healthcare, the biggest military budget. It seems that the greatest product that the U.S. is capable of producing today is war, and this makes us a very dangerous country. Our primary role in the global community is as a mercenary army in the interests of big business.

The So-Called Free Market

The hyper-consumerist culture of the U.S. has led to predatory lending and credit schemes that have put millions of people in the U.S. on the brink of bankruptcy, and the sacking of the Global South for exploited, under-paid workers and natural resources to make cheap products. The U.S. population represents 6% of the world's population, yet consumes 30% of the world's resources and produces the greatest amount of carbon pollution.

The U.S. population represents 6% of the world's population, yet consumes 30% of the world's resources.

And while we're at it let's just be clear that the free market capitalism we have seen in the U.S. is by no means "free." In reality the U.S. economy functions as a form of socialism for the rich. Taxpayers have bailed out the savings and loan industry, banks, and airlines. We finance at least 2 federal social security programs: the one to which most of us contribute through each paycheck, and the one for United Airlines employees (since that company no longer pays its pension obligations). We give huge government contracts to the prison and military industrial complexes, and increasingly to private education and healthcare companies.

The "land of the free" is also one of only two countries in the world building walls between themselves and their neighbors (the other being Israel). This fortress mentality is a telling sign of an empire in decline. At a time when the U.S. population needs to be reaching out to the rest of the world more than ever, our government leaders are circling the wagons.

The Chicago Boys and their friends have made a terrible mess, and we haven't even touched on the destruction caused by unchecked industrialization, gutted environmental regulations, and the addiction to fossil fuels that have pushed life on the planet to the edge of oblivion. Fixing this disaster will take generations and a fundamental shift in the values and premises that we base our politics on.

A Cultural Shift

It's clear that a profound change in the U.S. political direction is necessary. A fundamental shift in the political and economic direction of the country will require a cultural shift and a redefinition of social and political relationships. We need to challenge the values of individualism and competition and the culture of consumerism and reintroduce key values in defining our economic and social relationships—values such as reciprocity, community, cooperation and solidarity. We need to affirm that as a society we share collective and community responsibilities. We must confront the underlying premises that have sustained the neoliberal/neoconservative agenda—namely that taxes, unions and government are all bad. As Donald Cohen [president of the Center on Policy Initiatives] has outlined, we need to assert that taxes, organized labor, regulations and government are in fact necessary to keep the greedy in check and to achieve a just and democratic society.

A significant political and cultural shift in the U.S. will also require us to redefine the "American Dream." The dream is not about a motivated individual being able to strike it rich. The dream that would benefit most Americans (including Latin Americans and Canadians) would be closer to the dream outlined by Dr. Martin Luther King, Jr. The dream should include racial, gender and queer liberation, meeting the basic needs of everyone in the community, and achieving peace in our local and global community.

We need to challenge the values of individualism and competition and the culture of consumerism.

In the *Story of Stuff* (storyofstuff.com) Annie Leonard beautifully explains the cycle of production and consumption that is driving the planet toward self-destruction. She describes how the values of consumerism were engineered during the 1950s and have become part of our social DNA today. Consumerism was designed as a deliberate political strategy, and must be challenged by a deliberate political strategy. The cycle of consumption is sustained by externalizing costs by exploiting communities for cheap raw materials and labor. Challenging this model will mean supporting the struggles of exploited and displaced communities and their right to organize.

Consumerist Capitalism Needs Fundamental Change

Benjamin R. Barber

Benjamin R. Barber is a senior fellow at Demos, a non-partisan public policy research and advocacy organization, and author of Consumed: How Markets Corrupt Children, Infantilize Adults, and Swallow Citizens Whole.

As America, recession mired, enters the hope-inspired age of [President] Barack Obama, a silent but fateful struggle for the soul of capitalism is being waged. Can the market system finally be made to serve us? Or will we continue to serve it? [Former President] George W. Bush argued that the crisis is "not a failure of the free-market system, and the answer is not to try to reinvent that system." But while it is going too far to declare that capitalism is dead, [American businessman and philanthropist] George Soros is right when he says that "there is something fundamentally wrong" with the market theory that stands behind the global economy, a "defect" that is "inherent in the system."

Confronting Consumerism

The issue is not the death of capitalism but what kind of capitalism—standing in which relationship to culture, to democracy and to life? President Obama's Rubinite [successors and allies of businessman and former Secretary of the Treasury Robert Rubin] economic team seems designed to reassure rather than innovate, its members set to fix what they broke. But even if they succeed, will they do more than merely restore capitalism to the *status quo ante*, resurrecting all the defects that led to the current debacle?

Being economists, even the progressive critics missing from the Obama economic team continue to think inside the economic box. Yes, bankers and politicians agree that there must be more regulatory oversight, a greater government equity stake in bailouts and some considerable warming of the frozen credit pump. A very large stimulus package with a welcome focus on the environment, alternative energy, infrastructure and job creation is in the offing [January 2009]—a good thing indeed.

It is precisely in confronting the paradox of consumerism that the struggle for capitalism's soul needs to be waged.

But it is hard to discern any movement toward a wholesale rethinking of the dominant role of the market in our society. No one is questioning the impulse to rehabilitate the consumer market as the driver of American commerce. Or to keep commerce as the foundation of American public and private life, even at the cost of rendering other cherished American values—like pluralism, the life of the spirit and the pursuit of (nonmaterial) happiness—subordinate to it.

Economists and politicians across the spectrum continue to insist that the challenge lies in revving up inert demand. For in an economy that has become dependent on consumerism to the tune of 70 percent of GDP [gross domestic product, a measure of a country's economic health], shoppers who won't shop and consumers who don't consume spell disaster. Yet it is precisely in confronting the paradox of consumerism that the struggle for capitalism's soul needs to be waged.

A Revolution in Spirit

The crisis in global capitalism demands a revolution in spirit—fundamental change in attitudes and behavior. Reform cannot merely rush parents and kids back into the mall; it must encourage them to shop less, to save rather than spend. If there's to be a federal lottery, the Obama administration should use it as an incentive for saving, a free ticket, say, for every ten bucks banked. Penalize carbon use by taxing gas so that it's $4 a gallon regardless of market price, curbing gas guzzlers and promoting efficient public transportation. And how about policies that give producers incentives to target real needs, even where the needy are short of cash, rather than to manufacture faux needs for the wealthy just because they've got the cash?

Or better yet, take in earnest that insincere MasterCard ad, and consider all the things money can't buy (most things!). Change some habits and restore the balance between body and spirit. Refashion the cultural ethos by taking culture seriously. The arts play a large role in fostering the noncommercial aspects of society. It's time, finally, for a cabinet-level arts and humanities post to foster creative thinking within government as well as throughout the country. Time for serious federal arts education money to teach the young the joys and powers of imagination, creativity and culture, as doers and spectators rather than consumers.

Recreation and physical activity are also public goods not dependent on private purchase. They call for parks and biking paths rather than multiplexes and malls. Speaking of the multiplex, why has the new communications technology been left almost entirely to commerce? Its architecture is democratic, and its networking potential is deeply social. Yet for the most part, it has been put to private and commercial rather than educational and cultural uses. Its democratic and artistic possibilities need to be elaborated, even subsidized.

The Cost of Transformation

Of course, much of what is required cannot be leveraged by government policy alone, or by a stimulus package and new regulations over the securities and banking markets. A cultural ethos is at stake. For far too long our primary institutions—

from education and advertising to politics and entertainment—have prized consumerism above everything else, even at the price of infantilizing society. If spirit is to have a chance, they must join the revolution.

The good news is, people are already spending less, earning before buying . . . and feeling relieved at the shopping quasi-moratorium.

The costs of such a transformation will undoubtedly be steep, since they are likely to prolong the recession. Capitalists may be required to take risks they prefer to socialize (i.e., make taxpayers shoulder them). They will be asked to create new markets rather than exploit and abuse old ones; to simultaneously jump-start investments and inventions that create jobs and help generate those new consumers who will buy the useful and necessary things capitalists make once they start addressing real needs (try purifying tainted water in the Third World rather than bottling tap water in the First!).

The good news is, people are already spending less, earning before buying (using those old-fashioned layaway plans) and feeling relieved at the shopping quasi-moratorium. Suddenly debit cards are the preferred plastic. Parental "gatekeepers" are rebelling against marketers who treat their 4-year-olds as consumers-to-be. Adults are questioning brand identities and the infantilization of their tastes. They are out in front of the politicians, who still seem addicted to credit as a cure-all for the economic crisis.

Idealism Is the New Realism

And Barack Obama? We elected a president committed in principle to deep change. Rather than try to back out of the mess we are in, why not find a way forward? What if Obama committed the United States to reducing consumer spending from 70 percent of GDP to 50 percent over the next ten years, bringing it to roughly where Germany's GDP is today? The Germans have a commensurate standard of living and considerably greater equality. Imagine all the things we could do without having to shop: play and pray, create and relate, read and walk, listen and procreate—make art, make friends, make homes, make love.

Sound too soft? Too idealistic? If we are to survive the collapse of the unsustainable consumer capitalism that has possessed our body politic over the past three decades, idealism must become the new realism. For if the contest is between the material body defined by solipsistic [egoism] acquisitiveness and the human spirit defined by imagination and compassion, then a purely technical economic response is what will be too soft, promising little more than a restoration of that shopaholic hell of hyper-consumerism that occasioned the current disaster.

The convergence of Obama's election and the collapse of the global credit economy marks a moment when radical change is possible.

There are epic moments in history, often catalyzed by catastrophe, that permit fundamental cultural change. The Civil War not only brought an end to slavery but knit together a wounded country, opened the West and spurred capitalist investment in ways that created the modern American nation. The Great Depression legitimized a radical expansion of democratic interventionism; but more important, it made Americans aware of how crucial equality and social justice (buried in capitalism's first century) were to America's survival as a democracy.

Today we find ourselves in another such seminal moment. Will we use it to rethink the meaning of capitalism and the relationship between our material bodies and the spirited psyches they are meant to serve? Between the commodity fetishism and single-minded commercialism that we have allowed to dominate us, and the pluralism, heterogeneity and spiritedness that constitute our professed national character?

The Possibility for Radical Change

President Obama certainly inspired many young people to think beyond themselves—beyond careerism and mindless consumerism. But our tendency is to leave the "higher" things to high-minded rhetoric and devote policy to the material. Getting people to understand that happiness cannot be bought, and that consumerism wears out not only the sole and the wallet but the will and the soul—that capitalism cannot survive long-term on credit and consumerism—demands programs and people, not just talk.

The convergence of Obama's election and the collapse of the global credit economy marks a moment when radical change is possible. But we will need the new president's leadership to turn the economic disaster into a cultural and democratic opportunity: to make service as important as selfishness (what about a national service program, universal and mandatory, linked to education?); to render community no less valid than individualism (lost social capital can be re-created through support for civil society); to make the needs of the spirit as worthy of respect as those of the body (assist the arts and don't chase religion out of the public square just because we want it out of City Hall); to make equality as important as individual opportunity ("equal opportunity" talk has become a way to avoid confronting deep structural inequality); to make prudence and modesty values no less commendable than speculation and hubris (saving is not just good economic policy; it's a beneficent frame of mind). Such values are neither conservative nor liberal but are at once cosmopolitan and deeply American. Their restoration could inaugurate a quiet revolution.

The struggle for the soul of capitalism is, then, a struggle between the nation's economic body and its civic soul: a struggle to put capitalism in its proper place, where it serves our nature and needs rather than manipulating and fabricating whims and wants. Saving capitalism means bringing it into harmony with spirit—with prudence, pluralism and those "things of the public" (*res publica*) that define our civic souls. A revolution of the spirit.

Is the new president up to it? Are we?

Current
CONTROVERSIES

CHAPTER 2

What Are
Some Concerns
About Capitalism?

Chapter Preface

There are many competing alternatives to capitalism, two of the most popular of which are socialism and communism. In assessing the advantages and disadvantages of capitalism, it is relevant to consider how a competing economic system might fare better or worse.

Capitalism's defining feature is the private ownership of capital, or the means of production. This means that nongovernmental private entities own the assets—the land, the resources, the buildings, the technology, and the knowledge—used to create goods and services. A key feature of capitalism is that people are free to sell their labor, for a wage, to employers. Thus, labor, assets, and goods are traded in the marketplace. Any wealth made by businesses after subtracting the cost of investment, production, and labor goes to the owners of businesses as profit. Proponents of capitalism celebrate the freedom and choice this economic system provides individuals. Opponents frequently criticize the wage system of capitalism as a form of exploitation.

Communism's defining feature is the public, or communal, ownership of capital. Unlike capitalism, there is no private property and no individual profit: the means of production are owned and utilized by all for the common good. Communists advocate egalitarianism, where all people labor toward a common good with no difference in wealth between them. Proponents of communism claim that such a system would eliminate the exploitation of some human beings at the hands of others for the goal of profit. Opponents of communism often contend that the system is unworkable because people need the motivation of profit to reach their full potential.

Socialism could be seen as an economic system that is hybrid of capitalism and communism. On the one hand, workers may work for a wage and may acquire wealth according to work done, similar to capitalism. On the other hand, the distribution of income is subject to social control by the government. Under socialism, the means of production are not privately owned, and one of socialism's defining features is the role the government plays in controlling the means of production by having a centrally planned economy. Proponents of socialism contend that it offers both a meritocracy to reward those who work hard, while also ensuring that all are provided for. Opponents of socialism often claim that the government's central role in socialism promotes inefficiency.

In reality, making a true assessment of each system is difficult, because it is nearly impossible to find pure examples of these economic systems in practice in any country. For example, capitalism usually operates with a certain degree of regulation and various kinds of social safety nets, communism never has existed in a purely egalitarian form, and socialism often exists with the corruption of government thwarting its stated goals. In addressing the potential problems of any economic system, it is worth considering the alternatives, as well as the possibility of blended systems. Some specific concerns about capitalism are addressed in this chapter.

Capitalism Is at Odds with Democracy

Michael Parenti

Michael Parenti is a writer, lecturer, and author of Democracy for the Few.

After the overthrow of communist governments in Eastern Europe, capitalism was paraded as the indomitable system that brings prosperity and democracy, the system that would prevail unto the end of history.

The present economic crisis [2009], however, has convinced even some prominent free-marketeers that something is gravely amiss. Truth be told, capitalism has yet to come to terms with several historical forces that cause it endless trouble: democracy, prosperity, and capitalism itself, the very entities that capitalist rulers claim to be fostering.

Democracy in the United States

Let us consider democracy first. In the United States we hear that capitalism is wedded to democracy, hence the phrase, "capitalist democracies." In fact, throughout our history there has been a largely antagonistic relationship between democracy and capital concentration. Some eighty years ago Supreme Court Justice Louis Brandeis commented, "We can have democracy in this country, or we can have great wealth concentrated in the hands of a few, but we can't have both." Moneyed interests have been opponents not proponents of democracy.

The Constitution itself was fashioned by affluent gentlemen who gathered in Philadelphia in 1787 to repeatedly warn of the baneful and dangerous leveling effects of democracy.

Michael Parenti, "Capitalism's Self-Inflicted Apocalypse," *Political Affairs*, January 22, 2009. Reproduced by permission of the author.

The document they cobbled together was far from democratic, being shackled with checks, vetoes, and requirements for artificial super majorities, a system designed to blunt the impact of popular demands.

In the early days of the Republic the rich and well-born imposed property qualifications for voting and officeholding. They opposed the direct election of candidates (note, their Electoral College is still with us). And for decades they resisted extending the franchise to less favored groups such as propertyless working men, immigrants, racial minorities, and women.

Moneyed interests have been opponents not proponents of democracy.

Today conservative forces continue to reject more equitable electoral features such as proportional representation, instant runoff, and publicly funded campaigns. They continue to create barriers to voting, be it through overly severe registration requirements, voter roll purges, inadequate polling accommodations, and electronic voting machines that consistently "malfunction" to the benefit of the more conservative candidates.

At times ruling interests have suppressed radical publications and public protests, resorting to police raids, arrests, and jailings—applied most recently with full force against demonstrators in St. Paul, Minnesota, during the 2008 Republican National Convention.

The Need to Dilute Democracy

The conservative plutocracy also seeks to roll back democracy's social gains, such as public education, affordable housing, health care, collective bargaining, a living wage, safe work conditions, a non-toxic sustainable environment; the right to privacy, the separation of church and state, freedom from compulsory pregnancy, and the right to marry any consenting adult of one's own choosing.

About a century ago, US labor leader Eugene Victor Debs was thrown into jail during a strike. Sitting in his cell he could not escape the conclusion that in disputes between two private interests, capital and labor, the state was not a neutral arbiter. The force of the state—with its police, militia, courts, and laws—was unequivocally on the side of the company bosses. From this, Debs concluded that capitalism was not just an economic system but an entire social order, one that rigged the rules of democracy to favor the moneybags.

Democracy becomes a problem for corporate America not when it fails to work but when it works too well.

Capitalist rulers continue to pose as the progenitors of democracy even as they subvert it, not only at home but throughout Latin America, Africa, Asia, and the Middle East. Any nation that is not "investor friendly," that attempts to use its land, labor, capital, natural resources, and markets in a self-developing manner, outside the dominion of transnational corporate hegemony, runs the risk of being demonized and targeted as "a threat to U.S. national security."

Democracy becomes a problem for corporate America not when it fails to work but when it works too well, helping the populace move toward a more equitable and livable social order, narrowing the gap, however modestly, between the super-rich and the rest of us. So democracy must be diluted and subverted, smothered with disinformation, media puffery, and mountains of campaign costs; with rigged electoral contests and partially disfranchised publics, bringing faux victories to more or less politically safe major-party candidates.

Capitalism vs. Prosperity

The corporate capitalists no more encourage prosperity than do they propagate democracy. Most of the world is capitalist, and most of the world is neither prosperous nor particularly democratic. One need only think of capitalist Nigeria, capitalist Indonesia, capitalist Thailand, capitalist Haiti, capitalist Colombia, capitalist Pakistan, capitalist South Africa, capitalist Latvia, and various other members of the Free World—more accurately, the Free Market World.

A prosperous, politically literate populace with high expectations about its standard of living and a keen sense of entitlement, pushing for continually better social conditions, is not the plutocracy's notion of an ideal workforce and a properly pliant polity. Corporate investors prefer poor populations. The poorer you are, the harder you will work—for less. The poorer you are, the less equipped you are to defend yourself against the abuses of wealth.

Most of the world is capitalist, and most of the world is neither prosperous nor particularly democratic.

In the corporate world of "free-trade," the number of billionaires is increasing faster than ever while the number of people living in poverty is growing at a faster rate than the world's population. Poverty spreads as wealth accumulates.

Consider the United States. In the last eight years alone, while vast fortunes accrued at record rates, an additional six million Americans sank below the poverty level; median family income declined by over $2,000; consumer debt more than doubled; over seven million Americans lost their health insurance, and more than four million lost their pensions; meanwhile homelessness increased and housing foreclosures reached pandemic levels.

It is only in countries where capitalism has been reined in to some degree by social democracy that the populace has been able to secure a measure of prosperity; northern European nations such as Sweden, Norway, Finland, and Denmark come to mind. But even in these social democracies popular gains are always at risk of being rolled back.

It is ironic to credit capitalism with the genius of economic prosperity when most attempts at material betterment have been vehemently and sometimes violently resisted by the capitalist class. The history of labor struggle provides endless illustration of this.

To the extent that life is bearable under the present U.S. economic order, it is because millions of people have waged bitter class struggles to advance their living standards and their rights as citizens, bringing some measure of humanity to an otherwise heartless politico-economic order.

A Self-Devouring Beast

The capitalist state has two roles long recognized by political thinkers. First, like any state it must provide services that cannot be reliably developed through private means, such as public safety and orderly traffic. Second, the capitalist state protects the haves from the have-nots, securing the process of capital accumulation to benefit the moneyed interests, while heavily circumscribing the demands of the working populace, as Debs observed from his jail cell.

There is a third function of the capitalist state seldom mentioned. It consists of preventing the capitalist system from devouring itself. Consider the core contradiction [the father of modern communism] Karl Marx pointed to: the tendency toward overproduction and market crisis. An economy dedicated to speedups and wage cuts, to making workers produce more and more for less and less, is always in danger of a crash. To maximize profits, wages must be kept down. But someone has to buy the goods and services being produced. For that, wages must be kept up. There is a chronic tendency—as we are seeing today—toward overproduction of private sector goods and services and underconsumption of necessities by the working populace.

In addition, there is the frequently overlooked self-destruction created by the moneyed players themselves. If left completely unsupervised, the more active command component of the financial system begins to devour less organized sources of wealth.

Of itself the free market is an amoral system.

Instead of trying to make money by the arduous task of producing and marketing goods and services, the marauders tap directly into the money streams of the economy itself. During the 1990s we witnessed the collapse of an entire economy in Argentina when unchecked free marketeers stripped enterprises, pocketed vast sums, and left the country's productive capacity in shambles. The Argentine state, gorged on a heavy diet of free-market ideology, faltered in its function of saving capitalism from the capitalists.

Some years later, in the United States, came the multi-billion-dollar plunder perpetrated by corporate conspirators at Enron, WorldCom, Harkin, Adelphia, and a dozen other major companies. Inside players like [Enron Corp. CEO] Ken Lay turned successful corporate enterprises into sheer wreckage, wiping out the jobs and life savings of thousands of employees in order to pocket billions.

These thieves were caught and convicted. Does that not show capitalism's self-correcting capacity? Not really. The prosecution of such malfeasance—in any case coming too late—was a product of democracy's accountability and transparency, not capitalism's. Of itself the free market is an amoral system, with no strictures save "caveat emptor" [literally, "let the buyer beware"].

The Financial Crisis

In the meltdown of 2008–09 the mounting financial surplus created a problem for the moneyed class: there were not enough opportunities to invest. With more money than they knew what to do with, big investors poured immense sums into nonexistent housing markets and other dodgy ventures, a legerdemain [sleight of hand] of hedge funds, derivatives, high leveraging, credit default swaps, predatory lending, and whatever else.

Among the victims were other capitalists, small investors, and the many workers who lost billions of dollars in savings and pensions. Perhaps the premiere brigand was Bernard Madoff. Described as "a longstanding leader in the financial services industry," Madoff ran a fraudulent fund that raked in $50 billion from wealthy investors, paying them back "with money that wasn't there," as he himself put it. The plutocracy devours its own children.

In the midst of the meltdown, at an October 2008 congressional hearing, former chair of the Federal Reserve and orthodox free-market devotee Alan Greenspan confessed that he had been mistaken to expect moneyed interests—groaning under an immense accumulation of capital that needs to be invested somewhere—to suddenly exercise self-restraint.

The classic laissez-faire theory is even more preposterous than Greenspan made it. In fact, the theory claims that everyone should pursue their own selfish interests without restraint. This unbridled competition supposedly will produce maximum benefits for all because the free market is governed by a miraculously benign "invisible hand" that optimizes collective outputs. ("Greed is good.")

Is the crisis of 2008–09 caused by a chronic tendency toward overproduction and hyper-financial accumulation, as Marx would have it? Or is it the outcome of the personal avarice of people like Bernard Madoff? In other words, is the problem systemic or individual? In fact, the two are not mutually exclusive. Capitalism breeds the venal perpetrators, and rewards the most unscrupulous among them. The crimes and crises are not irrational departures from a rational system, but the converse: they are the rational outcomes of a basically irrational and amoral system.

A Disaster from Capitalism

Worse still, the ensuing multi-billion dollar government bailouts are themselves being turned into an opportunity for pillage. Not only does the state fail to regulate, it becomes itself a source of plunder, pulling vast sums from the federal money machine, leaving the taxpayers to bleed.

Those who scold us for "running to the government for a handout" are themselves running to the government for a handout. Corporate America has always enjoyed grants-in-aid, loan guarantees, and other state and federal subventions. But the 2008–09 "rescue operation" offered a record feed at the public trough. More than $350 billion was dished out by a right-wing lame-duck Secretary of the Treasury to the biggest banks and financial houses without oversight—not to mention the more than $4 trillion that has come from the Federal Reserve. Most of the banks, including JPMorgan Chase and Bank of New York Mellon, stated that they had no intention of letting anyone know where the money was going.

Free-market corporate capitalism is by its nature a disaster waiting to happen.

The big bankers used some of the bailout, we do know, to buy up smaller banks and prop up banks overseas. CEOs and other top banking executives are spending bailout funds on fabulous bonuses and lavish corporate spa retreats. Meanwhile, big bailout beneficiaries like Citigroup and Bank of America laid off tens of thousands of employees, inviting the question: why were they given all that money in the first place?

While hundreds of billions were being doled out to the very people who had caused the catastrophe, the housing market continued to wilt, credit remained paralyzed, unemployment worsened, and consumer spending sank to record lows.

In sum, free-market corporate capitalism is by its nature a disaster waiting to happen. Its essence is the transformation of living nature into mountains of commodities and commodities into heaps of dead capital. When left entirely to its own devices, capitalism foists its diseconomies and toxicity upon the general public and upon the natural environment—and eventually begins to devour itself.

The immense inequality in economic power that exists in our capitalist society translates into a formidable inequality of political power, which makes it all the more difficult to impose democratic regulations.

If the paladins of Corporate America want to know what really threatens "our way of life," it is their way of life, their boundless way of pilfering their own system, destroying the very foundation on which they stand, the very community on which they so lavishly feed.

Capitalism Promotes Prosperity, Democracy, and Peace

Erich Weede

Erich Weede is a former professor of sociology at the University of Bonn, Germany.

By and large, there are two distinct intellectual traditions in social theorizing. One is normative. It addresses how people *should* live or how the social order *should* be arranged. Much of the human rights discourse belongs to this tradition. The other tradition attempts to analyze the world as it is. Within this second tradition theories are evaluated according to criteria such as falsifiability, compatibility with known facts, explanatory power, or predictive value. If one is interested in feasibility, and if one links rights with corresponding obligations, then the separation between these intellectual traditions is regrettable. Then it makes little sense to generate long lists of human rights without knowing whether or not they ever can be implemented.

In this article, I argue that a short list of merely "*negative*" or protective human rights, which can be implemented, is preferable to a long list of "negative" and "*positive*" or entitlement rights, because the fulfillment of the latter requires an infringement of the former. Indeed, only a narrow focus on negative rights is compatible with a free economy, which alone provides the means to fund the material well-being of the masses—the objective of positive rights. Funding entitlements, however, undermines the viability of a free economy and thus appears self-destructive. . . .

Erich Weede, "Human Rights, Limited Government, and Capitalism," *Cato Journal*, vol. 28, no. 1, Winter 2008, pp. 35–52. Copyright © 2008 by The Cato Institute. Republished with permission of The Cato Institute, conveyed through Copyright Clearance Center, Inc. This article has been excerpted and edited for this publication.

Negative Rights

Negative rights serve to protect the individual, his liberty, and his property from coercion and violence. Negative rights prevent others from undertaking some types of actions, but they do not oblige others to help one. In order to safeguard negative rights government has to be limited. The link between negative rights and limited government was already well understood long before the term "human rights" gained currency. In the late 17th century, [English philosopher John] Locke wrote:

> The supreme power cannot take from any man part of his property without his own consent: for the preservation of property being the end of government . . . wherever the power, that is put in any hands for the government of the people, and the preservation of their properties, is applied to other ends, and made use of to impoverish, harass, or subdue them into arbitrary and irregular commands of those that have it; there it presently becomes tyranny, whether those that thus use it are one or many.

The right to life certainly is a fundamental human right. It is a negative right since it only requires that others do not kill one. In this context, one should recall that about 169 million people have been killed by states or their governments in the 20th century. Communists and National Socialists established the most murderous regimes. Among the victims of communism, there are tens of millions of deaths from starvation after the coerced collectivization of agriculture in [Joseph] Stalin's Soviet Union or Mao's China. Although the 20th century suffered two world wars and other bloody wars, fewer people died on the battlefield or because of bombing campaigns than have been murdered or starved to death by their own governments. Whoever wants to protect human rights should therefore first of all focus on the necessity of protecting people from the state and its abuses of power.

Positive Rights

Positive rights or entitlements commit the state and its officials to undertake certain types of action—for example, to guarantee certain minimal standards of material well-being. The American Bill of Rights (1789) is limited to negative or protective rights, while the United Nations General Declaration of Human Rights (1948) and the European Union Charter of Fundamental Rights (2000) encompass both protective rights and entitlements. The trend from short lists of negative rights to long lists of negative and positive rights has been accompanied by a rapid and sustained increase in public spending in the West.

Positive rights or entitlements commit the state and its officials to undertake certain types of action.

Classical liberals, in contrast to people called "liberals" in 20th century America and "social democrats" in Europe, demanded the primacy of individual liberty and thereby of protective rights and limited government. Providing people with entitlements forces the state to curtail the negative rights and liberties of individuals. In order to fund entitlements the state has to tax (i.e., to take coercively from) some people in order to provide for others. Entitlements have to rest on coercion and redistribution—that is, on a greater restriction of negative rights or individual liberty than would otherwise be necessary. As the balance of achievements and victims of communism demonstrates, the attempt to provide entitlements did not prevent tens of millions of deaths from starvation. Actually, the attempt to provide more than negative rights resulted in something less: the lack of respect of negative and positive rights. As I shall argue, this association between the attempt to guarantee entitlements by a monopoly of coercion and central planning is causally related to the repeated failure to protect even the right to life. . . .

Liberalism, Prosperity, and Human Development

One should expect a positive relation between economic freedom (or an increase in economic freedom) and prosperity (or economic growth)—and that is what one finds. As expected, economic growth also contributes to important positive rights, such as reducing child hunger. Building on [Austrian and British economist Friedrich] Hayek's idea that economic freedom does not only improve the lives of those who enjoy it, but also of those who still aspire to it, and that economically unfree societies can benefit from the economic freedom of others, one can provide a deeper explanation of the "advantages of backwardness" than merely by pointing to the transfer of technology from advanced to less developed economies. . . .

Advanced societies are advanced because they established better institutions and property rights before less developed countries. This institutional head start contributed to technological progress. From this perspective, the Chinese economic miracle beginning with Deng's [Chinese Politician Deng Xiaoping] reforms could be explained by the increase in economic freedom within China, or "creeping capitalism" as well as by the "advantages of backwardness," which ultimately rest on earlier progress, economic freedom, and capitalism in the West. Our freedom or the West's focus on negative rights in the past is among the drivers of Chinese and Asian growth.

To sum up: One may demonstrate historically and econometrically that limited government and economic freedom contribute to prosperity. Only where the state protects the primacy of negative rights or individual liberty, or where it at least moves in the right direction, as China has done since Deng Xiaoping's reforms in the late 1970s or India since the early 1990s, can economies stand a chance of becoming prosperous enough so that positive rights or entitlements can be funded. Obviously, unfunded entitlements are worse than useless.

Economic Freedom, Prosperity, and Peace

Capitalist development contributes not only to prosperity but also to reducing the risk of war. From a human rights perspective, the avoidance of war is a paramount concern because the fog of war has frequently been used as a cover for human rights abuses and war crimes. Econometric studies are compatible with the following causal relationships between economic freedom, prosperity, and peace: Whether assessed by financial market openness, trade, or property rights, economic freedom contributes to peace. The more trade there is between two states or the more they are economically interdependent, the less likely military conflict between them becomes.

In addition to this direct effect of economic freedom on the avoidance of war, there is an indirect effect via prosperity and democracy that is well documented. The freer an economy is, the more prosperous it is likely to be. The more prosperous a country is, the more likely it is to be a democracy. Military conflict between democracies is extremely unlikely. Economic freedom and free trade—that is, the global expansion of capitalism and the corresponding catch-up opportunities for poor countries—constitute the beginning of the causal chain leading to democracy and peace, at least to peace among prosperous or capitalist democracies. Economic freedom and free trade also exert a direct pacifying impact. Therefore, it is preferable to call this set of pacifying conditions the "capitalist (or market-liberal) peace" rather than the "democratic peace.". . .

Capitalist development contributes not only to prosperity but also to reducing the risk of war.

The global expansion of capitalism to developing countries has rescued hundreds of millions of people from dire poverty, especially in Asia, and also has helped increase respect for human rights. Cross-national studies support the propositions that globalization—that is, trade openness or foreign direct investment—promotes human rights in less developed countries, including free association and collective bargaining rights, women's economic rights, and the avoidance of child labor as well as of forced labor. Since human rights also promote trade, there seems to be a virtuous circle in which some human rights—negative or physical integrity rights in contrast to welfare rights—and international trade reinforce each other.

There is no perfect market or perfect government, but evidence shows that improving market institutions contribute to improving people's economic and personal freedoms. Political reform is still necessary in China and other authoritarian regimes if human rights are to be protected and enhanced. Retreating from globalization and market-liberal principles, however, would be a step backwards. According to econometric studies, globalization does not undermine human rights but serves to spread them beyond the Western world.

Capitalism Causes Poverty

Tony Wilsdon

Tony Wilsdon is a labor organizer and community activist who frequently writes for the Socialist Alternative, a national socialist organization.

The horrific spectacle of tens of thousands of people stranded, and effectively abandoned, for days in New Orleans in the wake of Hurricane Katrina [in 2005] has shocked the nation and the world. With the death toll estimated to be in the thousands, the fact that class and race discriminated against the victims poses important questions about our society.

Poverty and Capitalism

News commentators and politicians have been at a loss to explain away these disturbing facts. The public is left to ask: How could such levels of poverty and desperation exist in the richest country in the world? How could the supposed 'model for the free world' have created such poverty and despair? . . .

The simple fact is, the creation of poverty is a product of our economic system. It is a necessary by-product of capitalism. It flows from the internal workings of the system, which allows a few rich owners of vast capital to extract the labor of its workers for a pittance.

The extreme polarization of wealth in the U.S. has been accelerated and exacerbated by the neo-liberal policies pursued by both major parties during the 1970s, 1980s, 1990s, and so far this decade. The fact that the presidential candidates for both the Democratic and Republican parties in 2004 never focused on the conditions in the inner cities is an expression of this.

Tony Wilsdon, "How Capitalism Breeds Poverty: The Brutal Logic of Neo-Liberalism," SocialistAlternative.org, September 18, 2005. Reproduced by permission of the author.

Cuts in Public Spending

The guiding philosophy of both political parties is rooted in the idea that making conditions good for corporate owners (investors) will provide for all Americans. Under this philosophy, called neo-liberalism, removing all laws that constrain business profits is considered beneficial to the economy and to the U.S. public. In other words, that means slashing government programs and laws which do not directly benefit owners of capital (i.e. the richest 0.1% of the public).

The creation of poverty is a product of our economic system.

The past 25 years have seen drastic, extreme, and devastating cuts in spending in all areas of life, whether for housing, schools, public hospitals, public transportation, the infrastructure, job programs, welfare, etc. For example, federal support for low-income people's housing was slashed from $32 billion in 1978 to only $5.7 billion in 1988. That's a decline of more than 80%, when adjusted for inflation. It has since been almost completely eliminated.

The refusal of the [George W.] Bush administration to spend money to repair the levees [in New Orleans] is only a very sharp example of the complete abandonment of infrastructure spending flowing from the neo-liberal model. A study by the American Society of Engineers in March 2005 described how cuts in funding for bridges, public transportation, dams, schools, the drinking supply system, etc. means that a whopping $1.6 trillion would need to be spent over the next five years to bring the nation's infrastructure up to date.

Funding has been slashed for education at the federal and state level. As a result, the literacy rate of the U.S. has dropped from 18th to 49th place among the world's nations. In a massive study conducted by the National Adult Literacy Survey, over 90 million adult Americans, nearly one out of two, were found to be functionally illiterate, without the minimum literacy skills required in a modern society. Forty-four million adults were found to be unable [to] read a newspaper or fill out a job application, while a further 50 million could not read or comprehend above the eighth grade level.

The past 25 years have seen drastic, extreme, and devastating cuts in spending in all areas of life.

Cuts to Taxes and Regulations

City, state, and federal politicians have gone on an orgy of cuts to taxes and regulations on the corporations and their rich owners. A big handout has been privatizing public services. This reduces taxes for the rich and allows them to directly profit from those services, resulting in demands for lower wages and cost cutting. This results in lowering the quality of services—that is few public hospitals, poorer quality public housing, further unemployment and lower wages for those in the community. All these are recipes for further inner-city poverty.

The policies of neo-liberalism have hit African Americans and Latinos the hardest. The consequences can be seen in New Orleans with the recent removal of housing projects under the program Hope VI. This resulted in 7,000 poor people, mainly African Americans, being thrown in the street to join the countless others looking for work, without even a roof over their heads.

This dismantlement of government programs and government spending has been a huge boom for the profits of corporations and the super rich who own the bulk of shares. Now the horrific social consequences of these actions have erupted to the surface. But this is only one part of the neo-liberal program.

An essential weapon in the neo-liberal assault has been the demand for free trade. Corporate owners want to be 'free' to operate in any community they want, based on who can guarantee them cheaper labor and less restrictions on profit-making. If that means abandoning whole communities and moving operations to a different region or country, so be it.

Low Wages

To boost their profits, employers have ruthlessly attacked wages, benefits, and working conditions. Both political parties collaborated in refusing to raise the minimum wage, resulting in tens of million of workers seeing their living standards drop below the poverty line. Restrictions have been increased on eligibility for unemployment benefits. Fewer and fewer workers now qualify for any unemployment benefits, resulting in tens of millions dropping off the rolls and forced to live without any income.

Inherent in capitalism has been the maintenance of a sizeable pool of unemployed workers living on the edge of poverty who are desperate for jobs. It keeps workers competing with each other to get jobs, allowing corporate owners to keep wages low. This was first described by Karl Marx, the founder of scientific socialism, as an essential weapon used by capitalists to keep down wages. When this political and economic system is judged by future inhabitants of the planet, this policy will be judged, correctly, as one of the greatest crimes against humanity.

There has been a massive shift in wealth from the working class to the capitalist class.

Former Wall Street executive David Driver summed it up well: "The United States is the most capitalistic of major industrialized nations. This is not because America is a leader in per-capita gross domestic product, per-capita income, or productivity growth, for it is not. America does, however, have one of the most pro-business, inequitable, and inhumane socioeconomic systems in the industrialized world ... It certainly does not benefit the average citizen, nor does it benefit the country as a whole."

Or, as John Hinderaker, a board member for the Center of the American Experiment, a conservative think-tank, said: "There's more opportunity in the American economy today than at any time in its history. It's important to point out that income inequality isn't a bad thing, it's a good thing." The viewpoint of the capitalist class couldn't be better put.

This neo-liberal attack has lead to a massive increase in corporate profits. Just from 1980 to 1995, corporate revenues rose 129.5%, corporate profits rose 127% and executive pay rose 182%. The richest 1% of the population now own more wealth than the bottom 90%. There has been a massive shift in wealth from the working class to the capitalist class.

Time for a Radical Change

The class and race issues brought up by this tragedy [Hurricane Katrina] show the desperate need for a radical change in U.S. society. The hundreds of thousands left abandoned in the poor areas of New Orleans without jobs, with crumbling schools, lack of public hospitals, and without any hope of getting them have given Americans a glimpse of the ugly underbelly of this system.

As an immediate first step, we need to enact a massive public works program to rebuild the region of New Orleans and other devastated areas of Louisiana and Mississippi. This should be done by offering jobs and, if needed, training to those who have been displaced. The millions of unemployed and underemployed in the region should also be hired. This work should all be done at a living wage, and with full union rights and benefits.

However, conditions in New Orleans are an extreme example of the dire conditions facing tens of millions of workers in other cities and regions of the country. We need to set up similar massive programs of public works in these other cities and regions. This would include work to rebuild the infrastructure, build quality public housing, hospitals, transportation, schools, etc. Reallocation of investment and the hiring of unemployed workers could create new productive industries and factories, which would provide for the needs of working-class people living in those communities.

Such a rebuilding of the economy could ensure every person in the country had decent housing, a guaranteed living wage, access to quality healthcare and child care, and security in their old age. Funding must also be made available to clean up environmental pollution, and to reallocate scientists to address the massive environmental problems related to global warming and work out a plan to reverse them.

Capitalism is a system designed to produce for private profit, not for public need.

An Alternative to Capitalism

We should be under no illusions that the capitalist system can do this. The sizeable period of economic growth of the 1950s and 1960s is over. It was based on the period of the explosive emergence of U.S. capitalism during the turn of the last century, and a temporary period of worldwide superiority of U.S. manufacturing in the aftermath of World War II.

Today, we see a world economic slowdown, with U.S. corporations shutting down production here in search of areas that produce higher rates of profit. The economic engine of jobs, which helped some workers in previous generations to get out of the ghettos, will not be reoccurring. The vast majority of jobs created under [Bill] Clinton and Bush have been low-wage jobs, which have replaced higher-wage jobs. Under the rule of capitalism, the majority of the public faces further sharp attacks on their living standards and quality of life, with a growing number being forced into dire poverty, homelessness, and destitution.

Capitalism is a system designed to produce for private profit, not for public need. It is only by taking decision-making out of the corporate boardrooms and placing them under the democratic control of the majority that the economy can provide for our needs. To do that, we need to bring into public ownership the largest 500 corporations and financial institutions.

If the assets of these giant companies were under our democratic control, then investment and resources could be democratically controlled by working-class people. Resources would be available to address our most pressing social problems and allocated to areas of most need.

To achieve this means breaking from giving any support to the two big-business political parties—the Republicans and Democrats. They are both fully implicated in creating the present mess we are in. We need to build a new political party to represent our interests as workers, the poor, and young people, and which points a finger at the real villains, the super-rich and the capitalist system.

Freed from control by corporate sponsors, this workers' party could put forward a program that addresses our needs. It would be able to end this system of capitalism, which has been responsible for enriching a tiny group of billionaires at a time of massive need and poverty. We could then create a new democratic socialist society, where the working-class majority would have the power rather than the 1% who are rewarded under this system.

Capitalism Has Lifted Billions Out of Poverty

Jonah Goldberg

Jonah Goldberg is founding editor of National Review Online, *where he is currently editor-at-large.*

It's an old story. Loving parents provide a generous environment for their offspring. Kids are given not only ample food, clothing and shelter, but the emotional necessities as well: encouragement, discipline, self-reliance, the ability to work with others and on their own. And yet, in due course, the kids rebel. Some even say their parents never loved them, that they were unfair, indifferent, cruel. Often, such protests are sparked by parents' refusal to be even more generous. I want a car, demands the child. Work for it, insist the parents. Why do you hate me? asks the ingrate.

Of course, being an old story doesn't make it a universal one. But the dynamic is universally understood.

The Lack of Gratitude for Capitalism

We've all witnessed the tendency to take a boon for granted. Being accustomed to a provision naturally leads the human heart to consider that provision an entitlement. Hence the not-infrequent lawsuits from prison inmates cruelly denied their rights to cable TV or apple brown betty for desert.

And so it goes, I think, with capitalism generally.

Capitalism is the greatest system ever created for alleviating general human misery, and yet it breeds ingratitude.

People ask, "Why is there poverty in the world?" It's a silly question. Poverty is the default human condition. It is the factory preset of this mortal coil. As individuals and as a species, we are born naked and penniless, bereft of skills or possessions. Likewise, in his civilizational infancy man was poor, in every sense. He lived in ignorance, filth, hunger, and pain, and he died very young, either by violence or disease.

Capitalism is the greatest system ever created for alleviating general human misery, and yet it breeds ingratitude.

The interesting question isn't "Why is there poverty?" It's "Why is there wealth?" Or: "Why is there prosperity here but not there?"

At the end of the day, the first answer is capitalism, rightly understood. That is to say: free markets, private property, the spirit of entrepreneurialism and the conviction that the fruits of your labors are your own.

Wealth Is Capitalism

For generations, many thought prosperity was material stuff: factories and forests, gold mines and gross tons of concrete poured. But we now know that these things are merely the fringe benefits of wealth. [Soviet leader Joseph] Stalin built his factories, Mao [Chinese leader Mao Zedong] paved over the peasants. But all that truly prospered was misery and alienation.

A recent World Bank study found that a nation's wealth resides in its "intangible capital"—its laws, institutions, skills, smarts and cultural assumptions. "Natural capital" (minerals, croplands, etc.) and "produced capital" (factories, roads, and so on) account for less than a quarter of the planet's wealth. In America, intangible capital—the stuff in our heads, our hearts, and our books—accounts for 82 percent of our wealth.

Any number of countries in Africa are vastly richer in baubles and soil than Switzerland. But they are poor because they are impoverished in what they value.

In large measure our wealth isn't the product of capitalism, it *is* capitalism.

The Complaints

And yet we hate it. Leaving religion out of it, no idea has given more to humanity. The average working-class person today is richer, in real terms, than the average prince or potentate of 300 years ago. His food is better, his life longer, his health better, his menu of entertainments vastly more diverse, his *toilette* infinitely more civilized. And yet we constantly hear how cruel capitalism is while this collectivism or that is more loving because, unlike capitalism, collectivism is about the group, not the individual.

These complaints grow loudest at times like this: when the loom of capitalism momentarily stutters in spinning its gold. Suddenly, the people ask: What have you done for me lately? Politicians croon about how we need to give in to Causes Larger than Ourselves and peck about like hungry chickens for a New Way to replace dying capitalism.

This is the patient leaping to embrace the disease and reject the cure. Recessions are fewer and weaker thanks in part to trade, yet whenever recessions appear on the horizon, politicians dive into their protectionist bunkers. Not surprising that this week [end of July 2008] we saw the demise of the [World Trade Organization's] Doha round of trade negotiations, and this campaign season we've heard the thunder of anti-trade rhetoric move ever closer.

This is the irony of capitalism. It is not zero-sum, but it feels like it is. Capitalism coordinates humanity toward peaceful, productive cooperation, but it feels alienating. Collectivism does the opposite, at least when dreamed up on paper. The communes and collectives imploded in inefficiency, drowned in blood. The kibbutz [a communal settlement in Israel] lives on only as a tourist attraction, a baseball fantasy camp for nostalgic socialists. Meanwhile, billions have ridden capitalism out of poverty.

And yet the children of capitalism still whine.

Capitalism Uses Disasters to Engage in Economic Engineering

Naomi Klein

*Naomi Klein is an award-winning journalist, syndicated colum-
nist, and author of* The Shock Doctrine: The Rise of Disaster
Capitalism.

Few ideologues can resist the allure of a blank slate—that
was colonialism's seductive promise: "discovering" wide-
open new lands where utopia seemed possible. But colonialism is dead, or so we are told; there are no new places to discover, no *terra nullius* [land belonging to no one] (there never
was), no more blank pages on which, as [Chinese leader] Mao
[Zedong] once said, "the newest and most beautiful words can
be written." There is, however, plenty of destruction—countries smashed to rubble, whether by so-called Acts of God or
by Acts of [George W.] Bush (on orders from God). And
where there is destruction there is reconstruction, a chance to
grab hold of "the terrible barrenness," as a UN [United Na-
tions] official recently described the devastation in Aceh [site
of 2004 tsunami], and fill it with the most perfect, beautiful
plans.

Countries Under Reconstruction

"We used to have vulgar colonialism," says Shalmali Guttal, a
Bangalore-based researcher with Focus on the Global South.
"Now we have sophisticated colonialism, and they call it
'reconstruction.'"

It certainly seems that ever-larger portions of the globe are
under active reconstruction: being rebuilt by a parallel govern-

ment made up of a familiar cast of for-profit consulting firms, engineering companies, mega-NGOs [non-governmental organizations], government and UN aid agencies and international financial institutions. And from the people living in these reconstruction sites—Iraq to Aceh, Afghanistan to Haiti—a similar chorus of complaints can be heard. The work is far too slow, if it is happening at all. Foreign consultants live high on cost-plus expense accounts and thousand-dollar-a-day salaries, while locals are shut out of much-needed jobs, training and decision-making. Expert "democracy builders" lecture governments on the importance of transparency and "good governance," yet most contractors and NGOs refuse to open their books to those same governments, let alone give them control over how their aid money is spent.

Three months after the tsunami hit Aceh, the *New York Times* ran a distressing story reporting that "almost nothing seems to have been done to begin repairs and rebuilding." The dispatch could easily have come from Iraq, where, as the *Los Angeles Times* just reported, all of [engineering company] Bechtel's allegedly rebuilt water plants have started to break down, one more in an endless litany of reconstruction screwups. It could also have come from Afghanistan, where President Hamid Karzai recently blasted "corrupt, wasteful and unaccountable" foreign contractors for "squandering the precious resources that Afghanistan received in aid." Or from Sri Lanka, where 600,000 people who lost their homes in the tsunami are still languishing in temporary camps. One hundred days after the giant waves hit, Herman Kumara, head of the National Fisheries Solidarity Movement in Negombo, Sri Lanka, sent out a desperate e-mail to colleagues around the world. "The funds received for the benefit of the victims are directed to the benefit of the privileged few, not to the real victims," he wrote. "Our voices are not heard and not allowed to be voiced."

Rebuilding Is Not the Purpose

But if the reconstruction industry is stunningly inept at rebuilding, that may be because rebuilding is not its primary purpose. According to Guttal, "It's not reconstruction at all—it's about reshaping everything." If anything, the stories of corruption and incompetence serve to mask this deeper scandal: the rise of a predatory form of disaster capitalism that uses the desperation and fear created by catastrophe to engage in radical social and economic engineering. And on this front, the reconstruction industry works so quickly and efficiently that the privatizations and land grabs are usually locked in before the local population knows what hit them. Kumara, in another e-mail, warns that Sri Lanka is now facing "a second tsunami of corporate globalization and militarization," potentially even more devastating than the first. "We see this as a plan of action amidst the tsunami crisis to hand over the sea and the coast to foreign corporations and tourism, with military assistance from the US Marines."

It certainly seems that ever-larger portions of the globe are under active reconstruction.

As Deputy Defense Secretary, Paul Wolfowitz designed and oversaw a strikingly similar project in Iraq: The fires were still burning in Baghdad when US occupation officials rewrote the investment laws and announced that the country's state-owned companies would be privatized. Some have pointed to this track record to argue that Wolfowitz is unfit to lead the World Bank; in fact, nothing could have prepared him better for his new job. In Iraq, Wolfowitz was just doing what the World Bank is already doing in virtually every war-torn and disaster-struck country in the world—albeit with fewer bureaucratic niceties and more ideological bravado.

"Post-conflict" countries now receive 20–25 percent of the World Bank's total lending, up from 16 percent in 1998—itself an 800 percent increase since 1980, according to a Congressional Research Service study. Rapid response to wars and natural disasters has traditionally been the domain of United Nations agencies, which worked with NGOs to provide emergency aid, build temporary housing and the like. But now reconstruction work has been revealed as a tremendously lucrative industry, too important to be left to the do-gooders at the UN. So today it is the World Bank, already devoted to the principle of poverty-alleviation through profit-making, that leads the charge.

The stories of corruption and incompetence serve to mask this deeper scandal: the rise of a predatory form of disaster capitalism.

Profits in Reconstruction

And there is no doubt that there are profits to be made in the reconstruction business. There are massive engineering and supplies contracts ($10 billion to Halliburton in Iraq and Afghanistan alone); "democracy building" has exploded into a $2 billion industry; and times have never been better for public-sector consultants—the private firms that advise governments on selling off their assets, often running government services themselves as subcontractors. (Bearing Point, the favored of these firms in the United States, reported that the revenues for its "public services" division "had quadrupled in just five years," and the profits are huge: $342 million in 2002—a profit margin of 35 percent.)

But shattered countries are attractive to the World Bank for another reason: They take orders well. After a cataclysmic event, governments will usually do whatever it takes to get aid dollars—even if it means racking up huge debts and agreeing to sweeping policy reforms. And with the local population struggling to find shelter and food, political organizing against privatization can seem like an unimaginable luxury.

Even better from the bank's perspective, many war-ravaged countries are in states of "limited sovereignty": They are considered too unstable and unskilled to manage the aid money pouring in, so it is often put in a trust fund managed by the World Bank. This is the case in East Timor, where the bank doles out money to the government as long as it shows it is spending responsibly. Apparently, this means slashing public-sector jobs (Timor's government is half the size it was under Indonesian occupation) but lavishing aid money on foreign consultants the bank insists the government hire (researcher Ben Moxham writes, "In one government department, a single international consultant earns in one month the same as his twenty Timorese colleagues earn together in an entire year").

After a cataclysmic event, governments will usually do whatever it takes to get aid dollars.

Privatization

In Afghanistan, where the World Bank also administers the country's aid through a trust fund, it has already managed to privatize healthcare by refusing to give funds to the Ministry of Health to build hospitals. Instead it funnels money directly to NGOs, which are running their own private health clinics on three-year contracts. It has also mandated "an increased role for the private sector" in the water system, telecommunications, oil, gas and mining and directed the government to "withdraw" from the electricity sector and leave it to "foreign private investors." These profound transformations of Afghan society were never debated or reported on, because few outside the bank know they took place: The changes were buried deep in a "technical annex" attached to a grant providing

"emergency" aid to Afghanistan's war-torn infrastructure—
two years before the country had an elected government.

It has been much the same story in Haiti, following the
ouster of President Jean-Bertrand Aristide. In exchange for a
$61 million loan, the bank is requiring "public-private part-
nership and governance in the education and health sectors,"
according to bank documents—that is private companies running schools and hospitals. Roger Noriega, US Assistant Secretary of State for Western Hemisphere Affairs, has made it clear
that the Bush Administration shares these goals. "We will also
encourage the government of Haiti to move forward, at the
appropriate time, with restructuring and privatization of some
public sector enterprises," he told the American Enterprise Institute on April 14, 2004.

These are extraordinarily controversial plans in a country
with a powerful socialist base, and the bank admits that this is
precisely why it is pushing them now, with Haiti under what
approaches military rule. "The Transitional Government provide[s] a window of opportunity for implementing economic
governance reforms . . . that may be hard for a future government to undo," the bank notes in its Economic Governance
Reform Operation Project agreement. For Haitians, this is a
particularly bitter irony: Many blame multilateral institutions,
including the World Bank, for deepening the political crisis
that led to Aristide's ouster by withholding hundreds of millions in promised loans. At the time, the Inter-American Development Bank, under pressure from the State Department,
claimed Haiti was insufficiently democratic to receive the
money, pointing to minor irregularities in a legislative election. But now that Aristide is out, the World Bank is openly
celebrating the perks of operating in a democracy-free zone.

Shock Therapy

The World Bank and the International Monetary Fund have
been imposing shock therapy on countries in various states of

shock for at least three decades, most notably after Latin America's military coups and the collapse of the Soviet Union. Yet many observers say that today's disaster capitalism really hit its stride with Hurricane Mitch. For a week in October 1998, Mitch parked itself over Central America, swallowing villages whole and killing more than 9,000. Already impoverished countries were desperate for reconstruction aid—and it came, but with strings attached. In the two months after Mitch struck, with the country still knee-deep in rubble, corpses and mud, the Honduran congress initiated what the *Financial Times* called "speed sell-offs after the storm." It passed laws allowing the privatization of airports, seaports and highways and fast-tracked plans to privatize the state telephone company, the national electric company and parts of the water sector. It overturned land-reform laws and made it easier for foreigners to buy and sell property. It was much the same in neighboring countries: In the same two months, Guatemala announced plans to sell off its phone system, and Nicaragua did likewise, along with its electric company and its petroleum sector.

All of the privatization plans were pushed aggressively by the usual suspects. According to the *Wall Street Journal*, "the World Bank and International Monetary Fund had thrown their weight behind the [telecom] sale, making it a condition for release of roughly $47 million in aid annually over three years and linking it to about $4.4 billion in foreign-debt relief for Nicaragua."

Now the bank is using the December 26 [2004] tsunami to push through its cookie-cutter policies. The most devastated countries have seen almost no debt relief, and most of the World Bank's emergency aid has come in the form of loans, not grants. Rather than emphasizing the need to help the small fishing communities—more than 80 percent of the wave's victims—the bank is pushing for expansion of the tourism sector and industrial fish farms. As for the damaged public infrastructure, like roads and schools, bank documents recognize that rebuilding them "may strain public finances" and suggest that governments consider privatization (yes, they have only one idea). "For certain investments," notes the bank's tsunami-response plan, "it may be appropriate to utilize private financing."

Disasters as Opportunities

As in other reconstruction sites, from Haiti to Iraq, tsunami relief has little to do with recovering what was lost. Although hotels and industry have already started reconstructing on the coast, in Sri Lanka, Thailand, Indonesia and India, governments have passed laws preventing families from rebuilding their oceanfront homes. Hundreds of thousands of people are being forcibly relocated inland, to military style barracks in Aceh and prefab concrete boxes in Thailand. The coast is not being rebuilt as it was—dotted with fishing villages and beaches strewn with handmade nets. Instead, governments, corporations and foreign donors are teaming up to rebuild it as they would like it to be: the beaches as playgrounds for tourists, the oceans as watery mines for corporate fishing fleets, both serviced by privatized airports and highways built on borrowed money.

In January [2005, Secretary of State] Condoleezza Rice sparked a small controversy by describing the tsunami as "a wonderful opportunity" that "has paid great dividends for us." Many were horrified at the idea of treating a massive human tragedy as a chance to seek advantage. But, if anything, Rice was understating the case. A group calling itself Thailand Tsunami Survivors and Supporters says that for "businessmen-politicians, the tsunami was the answer to their prayers, since it literally wiped these coastal areas clean of the communities which had previously stood in the way of their plans for resorts, hotels, casinos and shrimp farms. To them, all these coastal areas are now open land!"

Disaster, it seems, is the new *terra nullius*.

Free-Market Capitalism Is Not Implemented Through Coercion

Johan Norberg

Johan Norberg is a Swedish writer and a senior fellow at the Cato Institute. He is the author of In Defense of Global Capitalism, *originally published in Swedish.*

In the future, if you tell a student or a journalist that you favor free markets and limited government, there is a risk that they will ask you why you support dictatorships, torture, and corporate welfare. The reason for the confusion will be Naomi Klein's book *The Shock Doctrine: The Rise of Disaster Capitalism.*

Klein's Argument

In a very short time, the book has become a 21st-century bible for anti-capitalists. It has also drawn praise from mainstream reviewers: "There are very few books that really help us understand the present," gushed *The Guardian.* "*The Shock Doctrine* is one of those books." Writing in *The New York Times*, the Nobel-winning economist Joseph Stiglitz called it "a rich description of the political machinations required to force unsavory economic policies on resisting countries."

Klein's basic argument is that economic liberalization is so unpopular that it can only win through deception or coercion. In particular, it relies on crises. During a natural disaster, a war, or a military coup, people are disoriented, confused, and preoccupied with their own immediate survival, allowing regimes to liberalize trade, to privatize, and to reduce public

Johan Norberg, "Defaming Milton Friedman: Naomi Klein's Disastrous yet Popular Polemic Against the Great Free Market Economist," *Reason*, vol. 40, no. 5, October 2008, pp. 54–59. Copyright © 2008 by Reason Foundation, 3415 S. Sepulveda Blvd., Suite 400, Los Angeles, CA 90034. www.reason.com. Reproduced by permission.

spending with little opposition. According to Klein, "neoliberal" economists have welcomed Hurricane Katrina [2005], the Southeast Asian tsunami [2004], the Iraq war, and the South American military coups of the 1970s as opportunities to introduce radical free market polities. The chief villain in her story is Milton Friedman, the economist who did more than anyone in the 20th century to popularize free market ideas.

To make her case, Klein exaggerates the market reforms in question, often ignoring central events and rewriting chronologies. She confuses libertarianism with the quite different concepts of corporatism and neoconservatism. And she subjects Milton Friedman to one of the most malevolent distortions of a thinker's ideas in recent history. . . .

Most classical liberal reforms happen in democracies, not dictatorships.

Economic Liberalization

Even though Klein is dead wrong about Friedman, she may well be right in her broader thesis that it's easier to liberalize in times of crisis, and that there is a close connection between economic liberalization and political violence. It's true that several dictators have liberalized their economies in recent years and that some of them have tortured their opponents.

But how strong is this connection? If we look at the Economic Freedom of the World statistics assembled by the Fraser Institute, a Canadian free market think tank; we find only four economies on the planet that haven't liberalized at all since 1980, so obviously reform has taken place in all sorts of countries. But the statistics clearly show that most classical liberal reforms happen in democracies, not dictatorships. Klein never talks about such rapidly liberalizing democracies as Iceland, Ireland, Estonia, or Australia, where reforms were given renewed support in several elections. Presumably these countries just aren't undemocratic and brutal enough. She does discuss Britain under Margaret Thatcher, but only to argue that Thatcher too relied on shocks and violence.

The Iron Lady won re-election in 1983, Klein says, because of the boost she got from the Falklands War. She doesn't mention another reason for Thatcher's growing popularity: The British economy was improving rapidly at the time. A 1987 study in the *British Journal of Political Science* looked in detail at the timing of events and British voters' perception of them, and made a strong case that the Tories gained only three percentage points from the war; the vast majority of the gain came from improved economic prospects. And the Falklands War certainly cannot explain why Tories won two more elections after that, nor why Tony Blair's New Labour had to dress itself in Thatcherite clothes to be elected.

Naomi Klein usually exaggerates the economic liberalization that has been carried out by brutal dictators. She needs to demonstrate that [Chilean dictator President Augusto] Pinochet's interest in market reforms was typical of authoritarian regimes—otherwise, her arch-villain Friedman might have been right when he said that the surprising thing in Chile was not that the market worked but that the generals allowed it to work. So Klein ropes in the Argentinean dictatorship of 1976–1983. Based on those two examples, she claims the southern part of Latin America is where "contemporary capitalism was born." She even calls the countries "Chicago School juntas."

Economic Reform

There were indeed advisers from the University of Chicago in Argentina; since there is strong global demand for Chicago economists, they have visited many countries. But their influence in Argentina was barely noticeable. In the Fraser Institute index of economic freedom, which gives scores from 1 (the least free) to 10 (the most), Argentina moved from 3.25 in 1975 to 3.86 in 1985. Compare this with the countries Klein mentions as superior alternatives to the Chicago Boys' brutal "neoliberal" models: Sweden went from 5.62 in 1975 to 6.63 in 1985; Malaysia, one of the "mixed, managed economies" Klein prefers, went from 6.43 to 7.13. In 1985, after Argentina allegedly applied Friedman's ideas, the country's economy was less market-oriented than all the Eastern European communist economies tracked by Fraser, including Poland, Hungary, and Romania. But Argentina tortured people, so in Klein's mind it must have been on the fast track to free markets.

By Klein's account, China is another country that violently imposed Friedmanite reforms. To make this case, she rewrites the history of the Tiananmen Square massacre of 1989, claiming the protesters were primarily opposed to economic liberalization, instead of one-party dictatorship. According to Klein, the Communist Party, led by Deng Xiaoping, attacked them to save its free market program and advance yet more sweeping reforms while people were still in shock.

The protests soon grew to include everybody who wanted liberal democracy—both those who wanted more economic reform and those who wanted less.

If the students were indeed protesting economic reform, they seldom expressed that grievance at the time. Instead, they demonstrated in favor of democracy, government transparency, and equality before the law, and against bureaucracy and violence. The protesters first gathered to mourn former Secretary General Hu Yaobang, one of China's most important economic reformers. The protests soon grew to include everybody who wanted liberal democracy—both those who wanted more economic reform and those who wanted less. Klein equates the second element with the whole protest.

No Shock Therapy

Chinese officials suppressed the demonstrations because they wanted to protect the party's power, not because they wanted to liberalize the economy. The majority were economic conservatives who were skeptical of markets; some even refused to visit Chinese free trade zones on principle. And the economic reforms did not accelerate after the massacre, as Klein claims. For the first time since their inception, they stalled.

The most consistent free marketeer in the leadership, General Secretary Zhao Ziyang, was purged because he supported the protesters, and he spent the rest of his life under house arrest. (Friedman had met him in Beijing in 1988 and wrote him a letter of advice. For Klein, this is yet another meeting with a tyrant.) Zhao's rivals—including Premier Li Peng, who was pushing for a violent crackdown on the protesters—then tried to roll the market reforms back and reintroduce economic controls. The conservatives blamed the unrest on the openness associated with economic liberalization, and Deng's position in the party was weakened. Far from being the start of "shock therapy," Tiananmen Square was almost the end of China's economic liberalization. Klein writes that "Tiananmen paved the way for a radical transformation free from fear of rebellion," but according to the Fraser statistics, China was actually less economically open in 1990 than it was in 1985.

Klein writes that Deng opened the Chinese economy "in the three years immediately following the bloodbath." This is true only if "immediately" means "three years later." Reform faltered so much in the years following the crackdown that Deng felt he needed to go outside normal channels and jump-start liberalization in the spring of 1992, even though he was 87 years old and had formally retired. His "southern tour" was a trip filled with speeches and networking aimed at saving the reform program. The tour was not initially reported in the national media, since they were controlled by Deng's rivals. Deng even found himself forced to write articles supporting his agenda under a pen name to get access. But he was eventually successful in winning local support and building alliances with provincial governors who favored liberalization. Only then did President Jiang Zemin reluctantly support Deng's reforms.

Far from being the start of "shock therapy," Tiananmen Square was almost the end of China's economic liberalization.

The Truth About Crises

To show that radical economic liberalization can happen only in dictatorships, Klein compares China to democratic Poland in the late 1980s and early '90s: "In China, where the state used the gloves-off method of terror, torture and assassination, the result was, from a market perspective, an unqualified success. In Poland, where only the shock of economic crisis and rapid change was harnessed—and there was no overt violence—the effects of the shock eventually wore off, and the results were far more ambiguous." Once again, the statistics tell a different story. According to the Fraser data, Poland actually took reform farther and faster. In 1985 its economy was much less open, with a score of 3.93 versus China's 5.11. In 1995, both scored 5.3. In 2005 Poland was way ahead, with 6.83 to China's 5.9.

Klein also exaggerates the free market elements in anything she can associate with a crisis. She writes that politicians used Hurricane Katrina to introduce "a fundamentalist version of capitalism" in New Orleans. The "fundamentalist" reform in question? The introduction of more charter schools. Not satisfied to exaggerate just the nature of the change, Klein also stretches its extent: She writes that the school board used to run 123 public schools but after the hurricane ran only four, whereas the number of charter schools increased from seven to 31. She doesn't mention that these figures date to the period immediately after the hurricane, when the school board was much slower to reopen its schools. As of September 2007, ordinary public schools again outnumbered charter schools, 47 to 44.

The strangest thing about Klein's suggestion that crises benefit free markets and limited government is that there is such a long record of the exact opposite. World War I led to communism in Russia; economic depression gave us Nazi Germany. Wars and other disasters are rarely friends of freedom. On the contrary, politicians and government officials often use crises as an opportunity to increase their budgets and powers. As one prominent economist put it while explaining his opposition to war in Iraq: "War is a friend of the state. . . . In time of war, government will take powers and do things that it would not ordinarily do." The economist? Milton Friedman.

Wars and other disasters are rarely friends of freedom.

Friedman was right about the Iraq war: The [George W.] Bush administration has used that conflict and the larger War on Terror to dramatically expand the federal government's powers and expenditures. Bizarrely, Klein points to the U.S. after 9/11 as a major illustration of her thesis. She claims the terrorist attacks gave the Bush administration an opportunity to implement Friedman's ideas by benefiting friends in the defense and security industries with new contracts and unprecedented sums of money. Klein never clearly explains how this could possibly be Friedmanite. In the real world, Friedman "had always emphasized waste in defense spending and the danger to political freedom posed by militarism," in the words of his biographer Lanny Ebenstein. Somehow, Klein has confused Friedman's limited-government liberalism with corporatism.

Nothing Against Free Markets

As Klein sees it, in Bush's America "you have corporatism: big business and big government combining their formidable power to regulate and control the citizenry." This sounds like a healthy libertarian critique of the administration—something Friedman himself might say. But Klein thinks that Bush-style corporatism is the "pinnacle of the counterrevolution launched by Friedman" and that the team that implemented it is "Friedmanite to the core."

So even when the U.S. government breaks all the rules in Milton Friedman's book, Klein blames Friedman. At one point she writes about the lack of openness in the Iraqi economy: "All the . . . U.S. corporations that were in Iraq to take advantage of the reconstruction were part of a vast protectionist racket whereby the U.S. government had created their markets with war, barred their competitors from even entering the race, then paid them to do the work, while guaranteeing them a profit to boot—all at taxpayer expense." This would be an excellent Friedmanite critique of how governments enrich their friends at the expense of competitors and taxpayers—if it weren't for the conclusion to the paragraph: "The Chicago School crusade . . . had finally reached its zenith in this corporate New Deal."

For Klein, tax-funded corporate welfare is the zenith of Chicago's free market revolution. The idea seems to be that Milton Friedman likes corporations, so if governments give corporations contracts, subsidies, protection, and privileges, that must be Friedmanite. At times it seems like Klein thinks any policy is Friedmanite if private companies are involved. But you would have a hard time finding an economist more persistent than Friedman in warning how corporations and capitalists conspire against the public to obtain special privileges. As Friedman wrote in *Reason* in 1978: "Business corporations in general are not defenders of free enterprise. On the contrary, they are one of the chief sources of danger. . . . Every businessman is in favor of freedom for everybody else, but when it comes to himself that's a different question. We have to have that tariff to protect us against competition from abroad. We have to have that special provision in the tax code. We have to have that subsidy."

In the absence of serious arguments against free markets, we are left with Klein's reasonable critiques of torture, dictatorships, corruption, and corporate welfare. In essence, her book says that Milton Friedman's limited-government ideals are bad because governments are incompetent, corrupt, and cruel. If there is a disaster here, it is not one of Friedman's making.

CHAPTER 3

Is Capitalism to Blame for the Global Financial Crisis?

Chapter Preface

With a global financial crisis in full swing by 2009, many experts have tried to determine the origins of the problem. For many the beginning of the crisis can be traced back to 2006, when what at first appeared as a small housing downturn ended up being the start of a large economic downturn that eventually affected the entire world. By the end of 2008, few doubted the existence of a global financial crisis. The questions of why it happened and what to do about it, though, are sources of much contention. Understanding what happened is an essential first step in determining whether capitalist economic policies caused the crisis.

Looking back there were signs of trouble starting in 2006 in the U.S. housing market. Interest rates for mortgages had been at historic low levels in the early twenty-first century. These low rates made it cheaper for people to buy homes, and the housing market flourished for several years. In 2006, however, house values began to decline, and interest rates began to rise. The drop in house prices continued into 2007, prompting the subprime mortgage industry meltdown.

Subprime mortgages were loans given to people with poor or little credit, to people with little to no down payment, and to people who could barely afford the mortgage payment. Such loans were risky for lenders, but with rising housing prices in the early part of the century, the risks of homeowners defaulting on the loans were mitigated by the continually increasing property values. But once housing prices began to fall, subprime loan recipients were the most at risk: They often had no equity in their homes and frequently had adjustable mortgage rates that were on the rise, thereby increasing their monthly payments and leading in many cases to foreclosure. Throughout 2007, the large number of subprime loan defaults affected banks all over the world, because these subprime mortgages had been sold to banks as part of investment packages.

Due to the banks' bad investments, including subprime mortgages, credit availability started to freeze up around the world in 2008. This credit crunch slowed down consumer spending globally. By the beginning of 2009, the situation had clearly developed into a worldwide recession. By the end of summer 2009, some were claiming that the bottom of the crisis had been hit and that a low recovery was beginning to occur. The low point will only be clear in retrospect but, regardless of when improvement begins, it will no doubt be a long time until a full recovery is made around the world. Understanding why the economic crisis occurred and how to address it is essential to a sustained recovery. Some blame capitalism for the crisis and advocate for a departure from a capitalistic system, whereas others claim that only capitalist principles can spur recovery from a crisis that was caused by straying too far from capitalism.

Capitalism Caused the Global Financial Crisis

Michael Heinrich

Michael Heinrich is a mathematician and political scientist in Berlin. He is managing editor of Prokla, Journal of Critical Social Science.

This crisis [the 2008–2009 international financial crisis] deserves a closer look. It began with an act of overtrading culminating with a burst of the speculative bubble. Ever since the Dutch tulip mania in the early 17th century, such crises of speculation have always run the same course: a particular asset (whether stocks, homes, or even tulip bulbs) continuously increases in its estimated value, which further stimulates demand for this asset, because everyone wants to share in the seemingly unstoppable rise in value. People use their own wealth, and ultimately take out loans, in order to acquire the object of speculation. Prices climb even higher on the basis of increased demand, which leads to a further increase in demand. But at some point the rise is exhausted. It becomes more difficult to find new buyers, and initial investors want to sell in order to realize their profit. The price of the object of speculation falls. Now everybody wants to get out of the market in order to avoid losses, which leads however to a further fall in the price of the object of speculation. Many who started speculating late in the game and bought at a high price now incur high losses. Since these losses are combined with a general slump in demand, such a speculative crisis can have effects on the entire economy. In principle, the course of such speculative crises is known these days even to those who participate in them. But it is never clear to participants exactly

Michael Heinrich, "The Current Financial Crisis and the Future of Global Capitalism," *MRZine*, translated by Alexander Locascio, September 6, 2008. Reproduced by permission of Alexander Locascio.

what phase of the speculation they find themselves in: more or less at the beginning, where good chances for making a profit still exist, or closer to the end, shortly before the bubble bursts. Everyone hopes to be counted among the winners, even if he or she knows that the crash is coming.

Subprime Loans

After the bursting of the New Economy bubble in the year 2000, the Federal Reserve lowered the federal funds rate from 6.5 to 1 percent between January 2001 and the middle of 2003 in order to stimulate investment through cheap credit. For two or three years, the federal funds rate was even lower than the rate of inflation. Falling interest rates also made the buying of homes attractive, and living in the privacy of one's home is a widely accepted goal among all social classes in the USA. Between the years 2000 and 2005 the amount of mortgages almost tripled. The strongly growing demand for homes caused real estate prices, despite increasing construction, to increase 10–20 percent per year, which enticed banks into granting increasingly risky loans. Purchasing prices were now financed up to 100 per cent, and equity was no longer required of buyers. Normally, banks only finance 60–80 per cent of the purchasing price, so that the bank has a security cushion and incurs no losses in case of a foreclosure sale of the house (as a consequence of insolvency on the part of the debtor). Even if the house doesn't realize the original purchase price through the foreclosure sale, there normally remains enough for paying back the loan, and the loss is incurred solely by the debtor. In the case of strongly rising real estate prices, bank managers believed that nothing could go wrong, and that the safety cushion was automatically provided by climbing prices. However, many homeowners used the climbing real estate prices to increase their loans in order to finance their personal consumption expenditures. The establishment of a safety cushion was therefore further postponed. Moreover, the banks began to issue so-called "Ninja" credits, which stand for "no income, no job, or assets" on the part of the borrower. Such loans constituted a big part of the "subprime" loans that are such a frequent topic of discussion these days. These are loans to borrowers who can't really afford the loans, which means that there is a high risk of default, which the banks make up for by charging extra high interest rates. Above all, such "subprime" loans are then resold by the banks, whereby they are rid of their worries concerning insolvent debtors.

In the case of strongly rising real estate prices, bank managers believed that nothing could go wrong.

Real estate loans of varying quality were bundled together in a relatively complicated way to serve as collateral for bonds that are given such beautiful names as "collateralized debt obligations" (CDO). These were then successfully sold to other banks and funds. Such bonds offered high returns on the one hand (since real estate buyers had to pay such high interest rates) and seemed on the other hand to be a relatively safe investment, since they were covered by real estate. In order to keep these transactions off the books of the purchasing banks and thus hedged by their own capital, so-called "Structured Investment Vehicles" (SIV) were founded, which acted as foreign subsidiaries. They refinanced the costs of these investments with short-term bond issues at much lower rates of interest than those of the speculative bonds collateralized by mortgages. In Germany, it was not only private banks that followed this method of legally evading the scrutiny of regulatory bodies, but also public banks such as the Landesbank Sachsen.

The Shift in Value

With the rise of interest rates in the USA between 2003 and 2006, the rise in real estate prices was slowed down, but the interest burden of mortgages rose, since in most cases variable rates had been stipulated. Most notably in the "subprime" sector, where the interest rates were already high, the number of loan defaults strongly increased. As a result, the number of foreclosure sales increased, which further beat down real estate prices. Now the rise in prices was no longer slowing down; at the end of 2006, prices started sinking.

With the increasing insolvency of real estate buyers, the bottom fell out of the interest revenues of the bonds based upon these mortgages, and with sinking real estate prices, the collateral of these bonds was also gone, and their prices fell. This forced the banks and funds that had bought these bonds to engage again and again in "value adjustments" of their balances, a process which probably still has not reached an end [as of September 2008].

Distinctive Features of the Crisis

The phenomena described thus far do not yet constitute anything unusual in the history of capital. The current crisis is notable because of the role the banks have played in it. In stock market crises, the losers are frequently the many small investors who put their nest eggs into stocks and who find themselves holding worthless paper after a crash or who are even in debt because they financed their stock purchases with loans. In the case of the American real estate crisis, the aggrieved parties are the banks and speculative hedge funds that bought the real estate loans (or bonds covered by the loans) from the issuing banks. Many insolvent homeowners have lost their savings, which they put into their homes, as a result of foreclosures. But at least the easy credit offered by the banks permitted a higher level of consumption over the years. This time, it wasn't small savers putting their meager capital into fly-by-night stocks, but rather banks financing the purchase of overpriced real estate and the consumption expenditures of homeowners.

The extent of the losses that individual banks have had to absorb (not just American banks, but also for example public and private German banks that took part in the ostensibly safe speculative transactions) is however not yet clear. Not only because banks are reluctant to make the extent of their losses public knowledge, but also because it is frequently the case that they are themselves not fully aware of the exact extent. When engaging in the purchase of the bonds covered by real estate loans, the banks blindly trusted the judgment of the so-called "rating agencies." But the highest quality "AAA" ratings were paid for by the very banks that issued the bonds, which was not necessarily helpful as far as the objectivity of the ratings was concerned. Since nobody knows exactly which bank is holding on to how many rotten loans or maybe even facing bankruptcy, distrust between the banks has grown, which in the last year has almost paralyzed interbank trading. In interbank trading, banks grant each other short-term loans without any formalities in order to ensure that business proceeds smoothly. But if one bank has to take into account that the other bank might be bankrupt tomorrow, the typical "over night" loan also becomes a risk. Bigger problems have been prevented so far only because central banks reacted with a quick expansion of their lending.

The distribution of wealth in the leading capitalist countries has shifted considerably to the benefit of capital and high-income individuals.

Shifts Within Capitalism

The enormous losses which have been the topic of discussion so far—at the end of April [2008], the banks had written off around 270 billion dollars, but the total could also end up being around 400–500 billion [as of June 2009, the International Monetary Fund estimates total write-offs in the United States,

Japan, and Europe to be more than $4 trillion]—are also an expression of the structural changes which have occurred within global capitalism in the last 30 years: since the global economic crisis of 1974/75 and the neo-liberal policies introduced as a result of it, the distribution of wealth in the leading capitalist countries has shifted considerably to the benefit of capital and high-income individuals. Real wages have risen only a little bit since then, the increase in social wealth has benefited almost exclusively those already possessing high-incomes and great wealth. A large amount of these income gains, as well as a part of increasing business profits, was invested in the financial markets, which successfully courted investors with increasingly novel types of speculative financial instruments (so-called "derivatives") since the sweeping deregulation of the markets in the 1970s.

Various "pension reforms," all of which have been instituted at the expense of state pension systems, have also led to attempts by many employees to improve their future pension payments through "pension funds," so that lower-income individuals also ended up investing indirectly in the financial markets. As a result of these developments, the volume of financial wealth has grown far more strongly in the past few decades than aggregate output. And there is a constant search for further investment opportunities for this enormous increase in financial wealth, which greatly stimulates speculation. . . .

New Forms of Regulation

Around 30 years ago, the era of Keynesianism ended: Keynesian economic policies [after the economist John Maynard Keynes—the theory that government must sometimes act to regulate the economy] that had been reduced to "deficit spending" were replaced by neo-liberal concepts that proceeded from the assumption that "the markets" are the best and most efficient entities for regulating the economy. Since the 1980s deregulation, flexibilisation, and privatisation occurred worldwide as much as possible. Today, financial markets most closely approximate the neo-liberal ideal of a free and flexible market: state regulations were radically cut back, and due to the nature of the objects being traded, time lags and transaction costs are minimal, the "impulses of the market" can therefore impose themselves without hindrance. But it is precisely these deregulated financial markets that have proven to be extremely unstable and prone to crisis. Even Josef Ackermann, head of the Deutsche Bank, had to recently admit that he no longer believes in the often-invoked "self-correcting powers of the market." And the International Monetary Fund [IMF], which up until now has obligated every developing country in need of credit to "more markets" (also and especially in the financial sector), has discovered in light of the financial crisis that the international financial architecture displays "dramatic shortcomings" and that more state control and regulation is necessary. But whether such regulation is actually coming soon is uncertain: Ackermann did not intend for his criticism to be understood as a plea for more state intervention. Instead, he presented a voluntary code of conduct which financial institutions should adhere to in the future. The proposals discussed by the IMF also remain extraordinarily vague. It's possible that a further crisis is necessary before a new regulatory wave can begin. But the period of naïve market euphoria seems to be over for now.

Even without the dreaded collapse of the financial system, the prospects of global competitive capitalism are anything but rosy.

Even if a new era of regulation for the financial markets is on the way, however, it will not make capitalism free of crises. When analysing capitalism, one has to distinguish between institutional arrangements that favour crises, and capitalism's fundamental tendencies towards crisis, which are rooted in the contradictory determinations of capitalist production on the one hand and capitalist circulation on the other hand. Institutional arrangements can be altered, and as a rule, crises tend to induce such changes. That the goal of capitalist production is profit-maximisation and that this is partially mediated by speculation, however, cannot be changed, or at least not without abolishing capitalism.

New Crises

There are also indications of new crises. The enormous rise in consumption in the last few years has led to climbing raw material prices and a current rise in the price of foodstuffs. In the case of rising prices and the expectations of a further rise in prices, speculative investment will increase, in which assets are purchased solely with the intent of selling them at a higher price. There are already conjectures that the price rise for crude oil and wheat is partially a result of speculative futures contracts, so that new speculative bubbles are emerging.

The rising price of foodstuffs has already had a considerable economic impact: in India and particularly China, they are fuelling the already high rate of inflation. The possibility cannot be excluded that the Chinese central bank will attempt to fight inflation with a rise in interest rates or with a tightening of the money supply, thus choking off the hitherto extraordinary rates—annual rates of 8–9 percent—of growth. Then the flip side of the multi-polar structures of global capitalism would become evident: an economic crisis in China would not just be a Chinese problem, it would be a problem for the entire global capitalist economy. Even without the dreaded collapse of the financial system, the prospects of global competitive capitalism are anything but rosy.

The Financial Crisis Shows the Failure of Financial Capitalism

Saskia Sassen

Saskia Sassen is professor of sociology and a member of the Committee on Global Thought at Columbia University. She is the author of A Sociology of Globalization.

The misnamed "Group of Twenty" (G20) meets in London on 2 April 2009 to discuss how to save the global financial system. It is too late. The evidence is in: we don't have the resources to save this system—even if we wanted to. It has become too big to save: the value of global financial assets is several times the size of global gross national product (GDP). The real challenge is not to save this system but to definancialise our economies, as a prelude to move beyond the current model of capitalism. Why should the value of financial assets stay at almost four times the overall GDP of the European Union, and even more of the United States. What do everyday citizens—or the planet—gain from such excess?

The question answers itself. To explore further the inner workings of the financial system that has brought the world to this predicament is also to glimpse a future beyond financialisation. The task the G20 should actually address is not to save this financial system but to begin to definancialise the major economies to a significant degree, so that the world can begin to move towards the creation of a "real" economy that delivers security, stability, and sustainability. There is much work to do.

Saskia Sassen, "Too Big to Save: The End of Financial Capitalism," OpenDemocracy.net, April 2, 2009. Reproduced by permission.

Primitive Accumulation

A defining feature of the period that begins in the 1980s is the use of extremely complex instruments to engage in new forms of *primitive accumulation*, with taxpayers' money the last frontier for extraction.

Finance has created some of the most complicated financial instruments in order to extract the meagre savings of modest households.

Global firms that outsource hundreds of thousands of jobs to low-wage countries have had to develop complex organisational formats, using enormously expensive and talented experts. For what purpose? To extract more labour at the cheapest possible price, including unskilled labour that would be fairly low in the developed countries as well. The insidious element is that millions of saved cents translates into shareholders' gains.

Finance has created some of the most complicated financial instruments in order to extract the meagre savings of modest households: by offering credit for goods they may not need and (even more seriously) promising the possibility of owning a house. The aim has been to secure as many credit-card holders and as many mortgage-holders as possible, so that they can be bundled into investment instruments. Whether people pay the mortgage or the credit-card matters less than securing a certain number of loans that can be bundled up into "investment products". Once thus bundled, the investor is no longer dependent on the individual's capacity to repay the loan or the mortgage. The use of these complex sequences of "products" has allowed investors to reap trillion-dollar profits on the backs of modest-income people. This is the logic of financialisation, which has become so dominant since the neo-liberal era began in the 1980s.

Thus in the United States—ground zero for these forms of primitive accumulation—an average of 10,000 homeowners have been losing their home to foreclosures *every day*. An estimated 10-to-12 million households in the US will not be able to pay their mortgages over the next four years [beginning in 2009]; under current conditions they would lose their home. This is a brutal form of primitive accumulation: presented with the possibility (which is mostly a fantasy, a lie) of owning a house, many people of modest income will put whatever few savings or future earnings they have into a down-payment.

Permanent Crisis

This type of complexity is aimed at extracting additional value from wherever it can—the small and modest *and* the big and rich. This too explains why the global financial system is in permanent crisis. Indeed, the term "crisis" is in some respects a misnomer: for what is happening is more nearly business as usual, the way financialised capitalism in the neoliberal era works.

The financialising of more and more economic sectors since the 1980s has become both a sign of the power of this financial logic and the sign of its auto-exhaustion. When everything has become financialised, finance can no longer extract value. It needs non-financialised sectors to build on. The last frontier is taxpayers' money—which is real, old-fashioned, not (yet) financialised money. . . .

The Limit of Capitalist Logic

The difference of the current crisis is precisely that financialised capitalism has reached the limits of its own logic. It has been extremely successful at extracting value from all economic sectors through their financialising. It has penetrated such a large part of each national economy (in the highly developed world especially) that the parts of the economy where it can go to extract non-financial capital for its own rescue have become too small to provide the amount of capital needed to rescue the financial system as a whole.

By way of illustration: the global value of financial assets (which means: debt) in the whole world by September 2008—as the crisis was exploding with the collapse of Lehman Brothers—was $160 trillion: three-and-a-half times larger than the value of global GDP. The financial system cannot be rescued by pumping in the money available.

The difference of the current crisis is precisely that financialised capitalism has reached the limits of its own logic.

This in turn explains the abuses of entire economies made possible through extreme forms of financialising. Before the current "crisis" erupted, the value of financial assets in the United States had reached 450% of GDP that is to say 4.5 times total GDP. In the European Union, it stood at 356% of GDP. More generally, the number of countries where financial assets exceed the value of their gross national product more than doubled from thirty-three in 1990 to seventy-two in 2006.

Moreover, the financial sector in Europe has grown faster than in the United States over the last decade, mostly because it started from a lower level: its compound annual growth rate in 1996–2006 was 4.4%, compared with the US rate of 2.8%.

Even capitalist economies—leaving aside assessments of whether this is the most desirable economic system—do not need an amount of financial assets that is four times the value of GDP. Thus even within a capitalist logic, giving more funds to the financial sector in order to solve the financial "crisis" is not going to work—for it would just deepen the vortex of financialising economies.

The Needs of the Financial System

Another way to portray the current situation is via the different orders of magnitude involved in (respectively) banking and finance. In September 2008, the value of bank assets amounted to several trillion dollars; but the total value of credit-default swaps—the straw that broke the system—stood at almost $60 trillion. That is a sum larger than global GDP. The debts fell due, and the money was not there.

More generally—and again, to give a sense of the orders of magnitude that the financial system has created since the 1980s—the total value of derivatives (a form of debt, and the most common financial instrument) was over $600 trillion. Such financial assets have grown far more rapidly than has any other economic sector.

The level of debt in the United States today is higher than in the depression of the early 1930s. In 1929, the debt-to-GDP ratio was about 150%; by 1932, it had grown to 215%. In September 2008, the outstanding debt due on credit-default swaps—a Made-in-America product (and, it should be recalled, only *one* type of debt—was over 400% of GDP. In global terms, the value of debt in September 2008 was $160 trillion (three times global GDP), while the value of outstanding derivatives is an almost inconceivable $640 trillion (fourteen times the GDP of all countries in the world).

These numbers illustrate that this is indeed an "extreme" moment—but, again, it is not anomalous nor is it created by exogenous factors (as the notion of "crisis" suggests). Rather, it is the normal mode of operation of this particular type of financial system. Moreover, every time governments (that is, citizens and taxpayers) have bailed out the financial system since the first crisis of this phase—the New York stock-market crash of 1987—they have given finance the instruments to continue its leveraging stampede. There have been five bailouts since the 1980s; on each occasion, taxpayers' money was used to pump liquidity into the financial system, and each time, finance used it to leverage. *This* time, the end of the cornucopia is near—we have run out of money to meet the enormous needs of the financial system.

The level of debt in the United States today is higher than in the depression of the early 1930s.

The Challenges

The implication of the foregoing is that two major challenges need to be faced:

- the need to definancialise the major economies

- the need to move out of the current model of capitalism.

Both will be difficult, but it will help to focus on some very basic facts. The current estimate of official global unemployment is 50 million; the International Labour Organisation calculates that 50 million more could lose their jobs as the recession deepens. These figures are tragic for those affected. They are also relatively modest (without minimising the human reality in any way) when set against the 2 billion people in the world who are desperately poor. But this raises the question: how many "jobs" would be created if there were a system that aimed at housing and feeding those 2 billion? The world would then need those 50 million currently unemployed to go to work—and another billion more workers into the bargain.

A New Social Order

If seen in this light, the financial "crisis" could serve as one of the bridges into a new type of social order. It could help all involved—citizens and activists, NGOs [non-governmental organizations] and researchers, local communities and networks, democratic governments—to refocus on the work that needs to be done to house all people, clean our water, green our buildings and cities, develop sustainable agriculture (including urban agriculture), and provide healthcare for all. This innovative order would employ all those interested in working. When all the work that needs to be done is listed, the notion of mass unemployment makes little sense.

The technology to underpin this work—in helping to eliminate diseases that affect millions, and to produce enough to feed all—has existed for several decades. Yet millions still die from preventable diseases and even more go hungry. Poverty has become more radical: no longer about having only a plot of land that did not produce more, today it means having only your body. Inequality too has intensified and taken on new dimensions, including a new global class of super-rich and the impoverishment of the traditional middle classes.

The history of the last generation confirms that the neoliberal form of market economy cannot deliver answers to these problems of disease, hunger, poverty and inequality— indeed it reinforces—them. Some mixing of clean markets and a strong welfare state has (as in Scandinavia) produced the best outcomes yet; but for most capitalist economies even to come near to this model would entail sweeping internal change.

In any event, the increase in the financialising of market economies over the last generation has further sharpened the negative effects of profit-maximisation logics. To move even a little in the direction of addressing the problems financialisation has created means entering an economic space that is radically different from that of high finance. The challenge is there for those attending the G20 summit in London—and for those outside the gates.

Too Little Regulation Caused the Financial Crisis

Jacob Weisberg

Jacob Weisberg is chairman and editor-in-chief of the Slate Group, a unit of the Washington Post Company devoted to developing Web-based publications. He is the author of The Bush Tragedy.

A source of mild entertainment amid the financial carnage has been watching libertarians scurrying to explain how the global financial crisis is the result of too much government intervention rather than too little. One line of argument casts as villain the Community Reinvestment Act, which prevents banks from "redlining" minority neighborhoods as not creditworthy. Another theory blames Fannie Mae and Freddie Mac for causing the trouble by subsidizing and securitizing mortgages with an implicit government guarantee. An alternative thesis is that past bailouts encouraged investors to behave recklessly in anticipation of a taxpayer rescue.

A Global Economic Meltdown

There are rebuttals to these claims and rejoinders to the rebuttals. But to summarize, the libertarian apologetics fall wildly short of providing any convincing explanation for what went wrong. The argument as a whole is reminiscent of wearying dorm-room debates that took place circa 1989 about whether the fall of the Soviet bloc demonstrated the failure of communism. Academic Marxists were never going to be convinced that anything that happened in the real world could invalidate their belief system. Utopians of the right, libertarians are just as convinced that their ideas have yet to be tried, and that they would work beautifully if we could only just have a do-over of human history. Like all true ideologues, they find a way to interpret mounting evidence of error as proof that they were right all along.

To which the rest of us can only respond, *Haven't you people done enough harm already?* We have narrowly avoided a global depression and are mercifully pointed toward merely the worst recession in a long while. This is thanks to a global economic meltdown made possible by libertarian ideas. I don't have much patience with the notion that trying to figure out how we got into this mess is somehow unacceptably vicious and pointless—Sarah Palin's view of global warming. As with any failure, inquest is central to improvement. And any competent forensic work has to put the libertarian theory of self-regulating financial markets at the scene of the crime.

Three officials, more than any others, have been responsible for preventing effective regulatory action over a period of years.

To be more specific: In 1997 and 1998, the global economy was rocked by a series of cascading financial crises in Asia, Latin America, and Russia. Perhaps the most alarming moment was the failure or a giant, superleveraged hedge fund called Long-Term Capital Management, which threatened the solvency of financial institutions that served as counter-parties to its derivative contracts, much in the manner of Bear Stearns and Lehman Bros. this year. After LTCM's collapse, it became abundantly clear to anyone paying attention to this unfortunately esoteric issue that unregulated credit market derivatives posed risks to the global financial system, and that supervision and limits of some kind were advisable. This was a very scary problem and a very boring one, a hazardous combination.

Disbelief in Regulation

As with the government failures that made 9/11 possible, neglecting to prevent the crash of '08 was a sin of omission—less the result of deregulation per se than of disbelief in financial regulation as a legitimate mechanism. At any point from 1998 on, Bill Clinton, George W. Bush, various members of their administrations, or a number of congressional leaders with oversight authority might have stood up and said, "Hey, I think we're in danger and need some additional rules here." The *Washington Post* ran an excellent piece this week on how one such attempt to regulate credit derivatives got derailed. Had the advocates of prudent regulation been more effective, there's an excellent chance that the subprime debacle would not have turned into a runaway financial inferno.

There's enough blame to go around, but this wasn't just a collective failure. Three officials, more than any others, have been responsible for preventing effective regulatory action over a period of years: Alan Greenspan, the oracular former Fed chairman; Phil Gramm, the heartless former chairman of the Senate banking committee; and Christopher Cox, the unapologetic chairman of the Securities and Exchange Commission. Blame Greenspan for making the case that the exploding trade in derivatives was a benign way of hedging against risk. Blame Gramm for making sure derivatives weren't covered by the Commodity Futures Modernization Act, a bill he shepherded through Congress in 2000. Blame Cox for championing Bush's policy of "voluntary" regulation of investment banks at the SEC.

Cox and Gramm, in particular, are often accused of being in the pocket of the securities industry. That's not entirely fair; these men took the hands-off positions they did because of their political philosophy, which holds that markets are always right and governments always wrong to interfere. They share with Greenspan, the only member of the trio who openly calls himself a libertarian, a deep aversion to any infringement of the right to buy and sell. That belief, which George Soros calls market fundamentalism, is the best explanation of how the natural tendency of lending standards to turn permissive during a boom became a global calamity that spread so far and so quickly.

Markets can be irrational, misunderstand risk, and misallocate resources.

An Immature View of Capitalism

The best thing you can say about libertarians is that because their views derive from abstract theory, they tend to be highly principled and rigorous in their logic. Those outside of government at places like the Cato Institute and *Reason* magazine are just as consistent in their opposition to government bailouts as to the kind of regulation that might have prevented one from being necessary. "Let failed banks fail" is the purist line. This approach would deliver a wonderful lesson in personal responsibility, creating thousands of new jobs in the soup-kitchen and food-pantry industries.

The worst thing you can say about libertarians is that they are intellectually immature, frozen in the worldview many of them absorbed from reading Ayn Rand novels in high school. Like other ideologues, libertarians react to the world's failing to conform to their model by asking where the world went wrong. Their heroic view of capitalism makes it difficult for them to accept that markets can be irrational, misunderstand risk, and misallocate resources or that financial systems without vigorous government oversight and the capacity for pragmatic intervention constitute a recipe for disaster. They are bankrupt, and this time, there will be no bailout.

Laissez-Faire Capitalism Is Not Responsible for the Financial Crisis

George Reisman

George Reisman is professor emeritus of economics at Pepperdine University and author of Capitalism: A Treatise on Economics.

The news media are in the process of creating a great new historical myth. This is the myth that our present financial crisis is the result of economic freedom and laissez-faire capitalism. . . .

Laissez-Faire Capitalism

Laissez-Faire Capitalism is *a politico-economic system based on private ownership or the means of production and in which the powers of the state are limited to the protection of the individual's rights against the initiation of physical force.* This protection applies to the initiation of physical force by other private individuals, by foreign governments, and, most importantly, by the individual's own government. This last is accomplished by such means as a written constitution, a system of division of powers and checks and balances, an explicit bill of rights, and eternal vigilance on the part of a citizenry with the right to keep and bear arms. Under laissez-faire capitalism, the state consists essentially just of a police force, law courts, and a national defense establishment, which deter and combat those who initiate the use of physical force. And nothing more.

The utter absurdity of statements claiming that the present political-economic environment of the United States in some sense represents laissez-faire capitalism becomes as glaringly obvious as anything can be when one keeps in mind the ex-

George Reisman, "The Myth That Laissez Faire Is Responsible for Our Financial Crisis," GeorgeReisman.com, October 21, 2008. Reproduced by permission of the author.

tremely limited role of government under laissez-faire and then considers the following facts about the present-day United States.

Under laissez-faire capitalism, the state consists essentially just of a police force, law courts, and a national defense establishment.

Government Spending and Interference

Government spending in the United States currently equals more than forty percent of national income, that is, the sum of all wages and salaries and profits and interest earned in the country. This is without counting any of the massive off-budget spending such as that on account of the government enterprises Fannie Mae [Federal National Mortgage Association] and Freddie Mac [Federal Home Loan Mortgage Corporation]. Nor does it count any of the recent spending on assorted "bailouts." What this means is that substantially more than forty dollars of every one hundred dollars of output are appropriated by the government against the will of the individual citizens who produce that output. The money and the goods involved are turned over to the government only because the individual citizens wish to stay out of jail. Their freedom to dispose of their own incomes and output is thus violated on a colossal scale. In contrast, under laissez-faire capitalism, government spending would be on such a modest scale that a mere revenue tariff might be sufficient to support it. The corporate and individual income taxes, inheritance and capital gains taxes, and social security and Medicare taxes would not exist.

There are presently fifteen federal cabinet departments, nine of which exist for the very purpose of respectively interfering with housing, transportation, healthcare, education, energy, mining, agriculture, labor, and commerce, and virtually all of which nowadays routinely ride roughshod over one or more important aspects of the economic freedom of the individual. Under laissez faire capitalism, eleven of the fifteen cabinet departments would cease to exist and only the departments of justice, defense, state, and treasury would remain. Within those departments, moreover, further reductions would be made, such as the abolition of the IRS [Internal Revenue Service] in the Treasury Department and the Antitrust Division in the Department of Justice. . . .

Government Regulations

To complete this catalog of government interference and its trampling of any vestige of laissez faire, as of the end of 2007, the last full year for which data are available, the *Federal Register* contained fully *seventy-three thousand pages* of detailed government regulations. This is an increase of more than ten thousand pages since 1978, the very years during which our system, according to one *The New York Times* article . . . has been "tilted in favor of business deregulation and against new rules." Under laissez-faire capitalism, there would be no *Federal Register*. The activities of the remaining government departments and their subdivisions would be controlled exclusively by duly enacted legislation, not the rule-making of unelected government officials.

The actual responsibility for our financial crisis lies precisely with massive government intervention.

And, of course, to all of this must be added the further massive apparatus of laws, departments, agencies, and regulations at the state and local level. Under laissez-faire capitalism, these too for the most part would be completely abolished and what remained would reflect the same kind of radical reductions in the size and scope of government activity as those carried out on the federal level.

What this brief account has shown is that the politico-economic system of the United States today is so far removed from laissez-faire capitalism that it is closer to the system of a police state than to laissez-faire capitalism. The ability of the media to ignore all of the massive government interference that exists today and to characterize our present economic system as one of laissez-faire and economic freedom marks it as, if not profoundly dishonest, then as nothing less than delusional.

Government Intervention Is Responsible

Beyond all this is the further fact that the *actual responsibility for our financial crisis lies precisely with massive government intervention*, above all the intervention of the Federal Reserve System in attempting to create capital out of thin air, in the belief that the mere creation of money and its being made available in the loan market is a substitute for capital created by producing and saving. This is a policy it has pursued since its founding, but with exceptional vigor since 2001, in its efforts to overcome the collapse of the stock market bubble whose creation it had previously inspired.

The Federal Reserve and other portions of the government pursue the policy of money and credit creation in everything they do that encourages and protects private banks in the attempt to cheat reality by making it appear that one can keep one's money and lend it out too, both at the same time. This duplicity occurs when individuals or business firms deposit cash in banks, which they can continue to use to make purchases and pay bills by means or writing checks rather than using currency. To the extent that the banks are then enabled and encouraged to lend out the funds that have been deposited in this way (usually by the creation of new and additional checking deposits rather than the lending of currency), they are engaged in the creation of new and additional money. The depositors continue to have their money and borrowers now have the bulk of the funds deposited. In recent years, the Federal Reserve has so encouraged this process, that checking deposits have been created equal to fifty times the actual cash reserves of the banks, a situation more than ripe for implosion.

Fictitious Capital

All of this new and additional money entering the loan market is fundamentally fictitious capital, in that it does not represent new and additional capital goods in the economic system, but rather a mere transfer of parts of the existing supply of capital goods into different hands, for use in different, less efficient and often flagrantly wasteful ways. The present housing crisis is perhaps the most glaring example of this in all of history.

Perhaps as much as a trillion and a half dollars or more of new and additional checkbook-money capital was channeled into the housing market as the result of the artificially low interest rates caused by the presence of an even larger overall amount of new and additional money in the loan market. Because of the long-term nature of its financing, housing is especially susceptible to the effect of lower interest rates, which can serve sharply to reduce monthly mortgage payments and in this way correspondingly increase the demand for housing and for the mortgage loans needed to finance it.

Over a period of years, the result was a huge increase in the production and purchase of new homes, rapidly rising home prices, and a further spiraling increase in the production and purchase of new homes in the expectation of a continuing rise in their prices.

The Federal Reserve

To gauge the scale of its responsibility, in the period of time just since 2001, the Federal Reserve caused an increase in the supply of checkbook-money capital of more than 70 percent of the cumulative total amount it had created in the whole of the previous 88 years of its existence—that is, almost 2 trillion dollars. This was the increase in the amount by which the checking deposits of the banks exceeded the banks' reserves of actual money, that is, the money they have available to pay depositors who want cash. The Federal Reserve caused this increase in illusory capital by means of creating whatever new and additional bank reserves as were necessary to achieve a Federal Funds interest rate—that is, the rate of interest paid by banks on the lending and borrowing of reserves—that was far below the rate of interest dictated by the market. For the three years 2001–2004, the Federal Reserve drove the Federal Funds Rate below 2 percent and from July of 2003 to June of 2004, drove it even further down, to approximately 1 percent.

The Federal Reserve also made it possible for banks to operate with a far lower percentage of reserves than ever before. Whereas in a free market, banks would hold gold reserves equal to their checking deposits, or at the very least to a substantial proportion of their checking deposits, the Federal Reserve in recent years contrived to make it possible for them to operate with irredeemable fiat money reserves of less than 2 percent.

The Federal Reserve's ultimate purpose was to stimulate both investment and consumer spending.

The Federal Reserve drove down the Federal Funds Rate and brought about the vast increase in the supply of illusory capital for the purpose of driving down all market interest rates. The additional illusory capital could find borrowers only at lower interest rates. The Federal Reserve's goal was to bring about interest rates so low that they could not compensate even for the rise in prices. It deliberately sought to achieve a *negative* real rate or interest on capital, that is, a rate below the rate at which prices rise. This means that a lender, after receiving the interest due him for a year, has less purchasing power than he had the year before, when he had only his principal.

In doing this, the Federal Reserve's ultimate purpose was to stimulate both investment and consumer spending. It wanted the cost of obtaining capital to be minimal so that it would be invested on the greatest possible scale and for people to regard the holding of money as a losing proposition, which would stimulate them to spend it faster. More spending, ever more spending was its concern, in the belief that that is what is required to avoid large-scale unemployment.

Malinvested Capital

As matters have turned out, the Federal Reserve got its wish for a negative real rate of interest, but to an extent far beyond what it wished. It wished for a negative real rate of return of perhaps 1 to 2 percent. What it achieved in the housing market was a negative real rate of return measured by the loss of a major portion of the capital invested. In the words of *The New York Times*, "In the year since the crisis began, the world's financial institutions have written down around $500 billion worth of mortgage-backed securities. Unless something is done to stem the rapid decline of housing values, these institutions are likely to write down an additional $1 trillion to $1.5 trillion."

This vast loss of capital in the housing debacle is what is responsible for the inability of banks to make loans to many businesses to which they normally could and would lend. The reason they cannot now do so is that the funds and the real wealth that have been lost no longer exist and thus cannot be lent to anyone. The Federal Reserve's policy of credit expansion based on the creation of new and additional checkbook money has thus served to give capital to unworthy borrowers who never should have had it in the first place and to deprive other, far more credit worthy borrowers of the capital they need to stay in business. Its policy has been one of redistribution and destruction.

The capital it has caused to be malinvested and lost in housing is capital that is now unavailable for such firms as Wickes Furniture, Linens 'N Things, Levitz Furniture, Mervyns, and innumerable others, who have had to go bankrupt because they could not obtain the loans they needed to stay in business. And, of course, among the foremost victims have been major banks themselves. The losses they have suffered have wiped out their capital and put them out of business. And the list of casualties will certainly grow.

Consumption of Home Equity

Any discussion of the housing debacle would be incomplete if it did not include mention of the systematic consumption of home equity encouraged for several years by the media and an ignorant economics profession. Consistent with the teachings of Keynesianism [after the theories of economist John Maynard Keynes] that consumer spending is the foundation of prosperity, they regarded the rise in home prices as a powerful means for stimulating such spending. In increasing homeowners' equity, they held, it enabled homeowners to borrow money to finance additional consumption and thus keep the economy operating at a high level. As matters have turned out, such consumption has served to saddle many homeowners with mortgages that are now greater than the value of their homes, which would not have been the case had those mortgages not been enlarged to finance additional consumption. This consumption is the cause of a further loss of capital over and above the capital lost in malinvestment.

A discussion of the housing debacle would also not be complete if it did not mention the role of government guarantees of many mortgage loans. If the government guarantees the principal and interest on a loan, there is no reason why a lender should care about the qualifications of a borrower. He will not lose by making the loan, however bad it may turn out to be.

It is government intervention, not a free market or laissez-faire capitalism, that is responsible in every essential respect.

A substantial number of mortgage loans carried such guarantees. . . .

What this extensive analysis of the actual causes of our financial crisis has shown is that it is government intervention, not a free market or laissez-faire capitalism, that is responsible in every essential respect.

The Free Market Did Not Cause the Financial Crisis

Thomas E. Woods Jr.

Thomas E. Woods Jr. is the author of nine books, including (most recently) the New York Times *bestseller* Meltdown: A Free-Market Look at Why the Stock Market Collapsed, the Economy Tanked, and Government Bailouts Will Make Things Worse, *a free chapter of which is available at www.TomWoods .com.*

No supporter of the market economy could have been sur- prised when the recent financial crisis was inevitably blamed on "capitalism" and "deregulation." The free market, we were told, was a recipe for financial instability. "Advocates of the free market must confront the fact that both the Great Depression and the current financial chaos were preceded by years of laissez-faire economic policies," wrote Katrina van den Heuvel, editor of *The Nation*, and author Eric Schlossel, in September 2008.

It is not enough to call this a distortion of the truth. It is a grotesque distortion, worthy of the Soviet politburo. The crisis is in fact the altogether predictable fruit of massive govern- ment and central-bank distortions of the economy. That may be why the free-market economists of the Austrian School were practically the only ones to have seen it coming.

There has been much discussion on right-wing radio and in the conservative press about Fannie Mae [Federal National Mortgage Association], Freddie Mac [Federal Home Loan Mortgage Corporation], and the Community Reinvestment Act (CRA), which have been described as forms of govern- ment intervention that contributed to the financial crisis. To a

Thomas E. Woods Jr., "Interventionism and Economic Crisis," in *Freedom Daily*, No- vember 2009, pp. 34–38. Reproduced by permission of the author.

certain extent that is all well and good: Fannie and Freddie enjoyed special government-granted privileges, along with an implicit bailout guarantee, that allowed them to become much more substantial actors in the secondary mortgage market than would have been possible in a free market. Furthermore, politicizing the lending process and cajoling banks into abandoning traditional standards of creditworthiness cannot make a positive contribution to the health of the banking industry.

But although there is no question that those factors exacerbated the problems that led to the crisis, they are not the primary culprits. Britain has also experienced a housing collapse, even though there is no British analogue of Fannie, Freddie, and the CRA. Moreover, no matter what encouragements these and other institutions may have given to home purchases, where did all the money come from to buy all those houses and drive up their prices so high so quickly?

We should instead focus on the Federal Reserve System, an institution few Americans know much about but which, in addition to systematically undermining the value of the U.S. dollar—which has lost at least 95 percent of its value under the Fed's supervision—gives rise to the boom-bust business cycle.

Hayek pinpointed the central bank's artificial creation of credit as the nonmarket culprit in the business cycle.

A Cycle Primer

Economist F.A. Hayek wanted to understand why the economy moved in a boom-bust pattern—why there was, in the words of the British economist Lionel Robbins, a sudden "cluster of error" among entrepreneurs. Why should the people the market has rewarded in the past for their skill at anticipating consumer demand suddenly commit serious errors and all in the same direction?

Hayek won the Nobel Prize for his answer.

Building on the insights of Ludwig von Mises, who first began to develop what is known as Austrian business cycle theory in his book *The Theory of Money and Credit* in 1912, Hayek pinpointed the central bank's artificial creation of credit as the nonmarket culprit in the business cycle. (Economist Jesus Huerta de Soto applies Austrian business cycle theory to cycles that occur in countries that have lacked a central bank in his treatise *Money, Bank Credit, and Economic Cycles.*)

To understand Hayek's point, which exonerates the free market, consider two scenarios.

Scenario 1. Consider what happens when the public increases its savings. Since banks now have more funds to lend (namely, the saved funds deposited by the public), the rate of interest it charges on loans will fall. The lower interest rates, in turn, stimulate an expansion in long-term investment projects, which are more sensitive to interest rates than short-term projects. (Think of the difference in the decline in monthly payments that would occur between a 30-year mortgage and a 1-year mortgage if interest rates came down by even 2 percentage points.)

Lower-order stages of production are those stages closest to finished consumer goods: retail stores, services, and the like. Wholesale and marketing are examples of higher-order stages. Mining, construction, and research and development are of still higher order, since they are so remote from the finished good that reaches the consumer. When people's consumption spending contracts, it is a perfect time for higher-order stages of production to expand: because of people's additional saving, there is relatively less demand for consumer goods, and the resulting contraction of lower-order stages of production will release resources for use in the higher-order stages.

Scenario 2 Government-established central banks have various means at their disposal to force interest rates lower even without any corresponding increase in saving by the public. (For more on this, see *The Mystery of Banking* by Murray N. Rothbard, or his shorter classic, *What Has Government Done to Our Money?*) Just as in the case in which public saving has increased, the lower interest rates spur expansion in higher-order stages of production.

The difference, though, is a critical one, and which guarantees that these *artificially* low interest rates will not yield the happy outcome we saw in Scenario 1. For in this case, people have not decreased their consumption spending. If anything, the low interest rates encourage further consumption. If consumption spending is not constricted, the lower-order stages of production do not contract. And if they do not contract, they do not release resources for use in the higher-order stages of production. Instead of harmonious economic development, there will instead ensue a tug-of-war for those resources between the higher and lower stages. In the process of this tug of war, the prices of those resources (labor, trucking services, et cetera) will be bid up, thereby threatening the profitability of higher-order projects that were begun without the expectation of this increase in costs.

As the workers in the newly expanded higher-order stages of production begin to spend their incomes, they spend according to the same saving-to-consumption ratio they did in the past. Their desire to save, and thereby to sustain all this long-term investment, turns out to be not as great as the distorted structure of interest rates led entrepreneurs to believe. It becomes ever clearer that society is not prepared to support the expansion of time-consuming higher-order stages of production. They do not wish to save enough resources to make the completion of all the new projects possible. The lower-order stages will win the tug of war. Expansion in the higher-order stages will have to be abandoned. Some of the resources deployed there will be salvageable; others will have been squandered forever or will be of little to no use in later stages of production.

Preventing Correction

The economywide discoordination that reveals itself in the bust is not, therefore, caused by the free market. To the contrary, it is *intervention* into the free market, in the form of distortions of the structure of interest rates—which are crucial coordinating mechanisms—that causes the problem.

As the boom turns into bust, the economy tries to readjust itself into a configuration that conforms to consumer preferences. That is why it is so essential for government to stay entirely out of the adjustment process, because arbitrary government behavior can only delay the necessary and healthy process. Wages and prices need to be free to fluctuate, so labor and other resources can be swiftly shifted away from bloated, bubble sectors of the economy and into sustainable sectors of the economy where consumers want them. Bailouts obstruct that process by preventing the reallocation of capital into the hands of firms that genuinely cater to consumer demand, and by propping up instead those firms that have deployed resources in ways that do not conform to consumer references. Fiscal and monetary stimulus do nothing to address the imbalances in the economy, and indeed only perpetuate them.

Most observers cheered in the months following 9/11 [2001] when it seemed as if Alan Greenspan had successfully navigated the economy through the dot-com bust at the cost of only a relatively mild recession. The man the *New York Times* identified as "the infallible maestro of our financial system" had lived up to the expectations of those who treated him with a distinctly creepy reverence. But all he had done was hold off the inevitable recession, and make the current downturn all the worse. The recession of 2001 was the only one on record in which housing starts did not decline. Thus people drew the false conclusion—amplified by the alleged experts, including Fed economists—that the housing sector is robust through thick and thin, housing prices never fall, a house is the best investment someone can make, and so on.

Because Greenspan would not allow the full correction to take place, clearing out entrepreneurial errors caused by his previous intervention, market actors persisted in their errors for years thereafter. With the economy having continued along its unsustainable trajectory all that time, the bust that inevitably came was that much worse. Although market decisions were distorted in countless areas of industry, it was housing whose disproportionate growth was most obvious in the most recent boom. Easy money by the Fed, combined with government regulations that made mortgage loans especially easy and attractive, gave rise to a housing bubble—in other words, an array of prices that were unsustainably high. Housing is a durable consumer good generally purchased with long-term financing, so it fits in perfectly with the Austrian analysis that artificially low interest rates give undue stimulus to long-term projects.

The very existence of a central bank such as the Federal Reserve aggravates—indeed, institutionalizes—moral hazard.

Moral Hazard

There has been much discussion of moral hazard in connection with the flurry of bailouts that began in 2008. "Moral hazard" refers to people's readiness to act with an artificially elevated level of risk tolerance because they believe that any losses they may incur will be borne by other people. Hence the bailouts will tend to make major market actors even less likely to behave prudently in the future, since if they believe they are likely to be considered "too big to fail," they have more reason than ever to believe that they will not be allowed to go out of business, and therefore that they may continue to make risky bets.

This critique is correct as far as it goes, but it overlooks the related problem that the very existence of a central bank such as the Federal Reserve aggravates—indeed, institutionalizes—moral hazard. Since there is no physical limitation on the creation of paper money, firms know that no natural constraint exists on the power of the central bank to bail them out of any serious trouble. (Even if the supply of paper should be exhausted, the monetary authority can always add zeroes to existing notes.) In our own case, financial commentators spoke of the "Greenspan put," the implied promise that the central bank would intervene to assist the financial sector in the event of a serious downturn. No one has a right to be surprised when market actors behave accordingly.

Arguments over regulation and deregulation by and large miss the point. According to Guido Hulsmann, in his valuable book *The Ethics of Money Production,*

> The banks must keep certain minimum amounts of equity and reserves, they must observe a great number of rules in granting credit, their executives must have certain qualifications, and so on. Yet these stipulations trim the branches without attacking the root. They seek to curb certain known excesses that spring from moral hazard, but they do not eradicate moral hazard itself. As we have seen, moral hazard is implied in the very existence of paper money. Because a paper-money producer can bail out virtually anybody, the citizens become reckless in their speculations; they count on him to bail them out, especially when many other people do the same thing. To fight such behavior effectively, one must abolish paper money. Regulations merely drive the reckless behavior into new channels.

One might advocate the pragmatic stance of fighting moral hazard on an ad hoc basis wherever it shows up. Thus one would regulate one industry after another, until the entire economy is caught up in a web of micro-regulations. That would, of course, provide some sort of order, but it would be the order of a cemetery. Nobody could make any (potentially reckless!) investment decisions anymore. Everything would have to follow rules set up by the legislature. In short, the only way to fight moral hazard without destroying its source, fiat inflation, is to subject the economy to a Soviet-style central plan.

Since 2007 the typical pattern has unfolded before our eyes: a financial crisis whose ultimate cause is the government's own central bank is blamed on anyone and everyone else, while the central bank itself is portrayed as our savior rather than the culprit. This version of events is then used to justify still more expansions of government power.

It is urgently necessary for Americans to inoculate themselves against the relentless propaganda on behalf of the government's version of the story. That's why I wrote my book *Meltdown* earlier this year: to set forth a persuasive free-market explanation of the crisis that laymen can understand and use. It spent ten weeks as a *New York Times* best-seller, but the *Times* has refused to review it. That, in turn, is about the best endorsement I could have asked for.

Altruism Caused the Financial Crisis

Richard M. Salsman

Richard M. Salsman is president of InterMarket Forecasting, Inc., an investment consulting firm based in Durham, N.C. He is the author of Gold and Liberty.

Government intervention is once again wreaking havoc on the U.S. financial system and the economic security of millions of Americans—a tragic replay of previous crises. In 2008–2009, for the second time this decade (the first being 2000–2002), the value of U.S. publicly-traded stocks has plunged by 50 percent—but this time with an additional plunge in the median home price, which has dropped 23 percent from its peak in 2007. Thus American households have suffered declines of $8 trillion and $4 trillion, respectively, in the value of their two key assets—stocks and homes—and a 20 percent drop in their net worth, from its recent peak. Meanwhile Washington policymakers have mired Americans in yet another recession, with declining output, stagnant income, and a rising jobless rate. The current recession is not yet as severe as many prior ones, but it will worsen if interventions intensify.

The Alleged Cause of the Crisis

Relative to past economic downturns, few financial institutions have faltered or failed amid the economic turmoil of 2008–2009, but those that have include some of America's largest and most famous names, such as Merrill Lynch, Bear Stearns, Lehman Brothers, Citicorp, AIG, Washington Mutual, Wachovia, and Countrywide Financial. Since last fall [2008],

Richard M. Salsman, "Altruism: The Moral Root of the Financial Crisis," *The Objective Standard*, vol. 4, no. 1, Spring 2009. Copyright © 2005–2009 *The Objective Standard*. All rights reserved. Reproduced by permission.

Washington has only further fueled a crisis that began modestly in 2007, by bypassing bankruptcy courts and instead bailing out or nationalizing these firms, or forcing healthy firms to absorb them (thereby weakening the healthy ones). Whereas since mid-2007 U.S. stocks generally are down 50 percent, those of large U.S. financial institutions have plunged 80 percent, the worst performance since the Great Depression. With every new government intervention in the sector, there has been only a quickening of capital flight and stock-price declines.

What caused the current financial crisis? If most economists, politicians, and commentators are to be believed, the cause is capitalism and its inherent greed. According to Democrat presidential candidate Barack Obama, "we excused and even embraced an ethic of greed"; "we encouraged a winner-take-all, anything-goes environment"; and "instead of establishing a 21st century regulatory framework, we simply dismantled the old one." As a senator last fall, Obama decried as "an outrage" the need for a bailout plan "to rescue our economy from the greed and irresponsibility of Wall Street" (and then promptly voted for it). GOP [Republican] presidential candidate John McCain said the financial crisis was caused by "greed, corruption, and excess," as Wall Street "treated the American economy like a casino." With the *New York Times* in December, President [George W.] Bush "shared his views of how the nation came to the brink of economic disaster," citing "corporate greed and market excesses fueled by a flood of foreign cash," concluding that "Wall Street got drunk." In his *New York Times* column, Paul Krugman, recipient of the Nobel Prize in economics in 2008, repeatedly blames the crisis on "deregulation" and free-market "dogmas." Alan Greenspan— who for twenty years headed the Federal Reserve as Washington's money monopolist and top bank regulator— told Congress last fall that "those of us who have looked to the self-interest of lending institutions to protect shareholder's equity, myself especially, are in a state of shocked disbelief," agreed that it was a "flaw" in his ideology, and called for still more government regulation—which led many journalists to declare, with glee, that "Greenspan Admits Free Market Has Foundered." The *Washington Post* traces the crisis to a U.S.-led "crusade to persuade much of the world to lift the heavy hand of government from finance and industry," to "spread the gospel of laissez-faire capitalism," and claims that this "hands-off brand of capitalism" only "sickened the housing market and allowed a freewheeling Wall Street to create a pool of toxic investments that has infected the global financial system."

Washington has only further fueled a crisis that began modestly in 2007, by bypassing bankruptcy courts and instead bailing out or nationalizing these firms.

Government Interventions

The usual greed-blaming, anticapitalist interpretations cited above have fueled massive interventions in the U.S. financial sector in recent months, including partial nationalizations. America's largest bank (Citigroup) and largest insurance company (AIG) are now effectively owned and controlled by the U.S. government, through the Federal Reserve and Treasury Department. Since October Washington has sunk nearly $500 billion of taxpayer funds into the shares of America's four hundred largest banks, failing and healthy alike—often against the will of senior management. By March 2009, the money sunk into America's ten biggest banks constituted 45 percent of their stock market value, twice the proportion of October 2008; in the process, politicians and bureaucrats have increasingly dictated the banks' policies on lending, dividends, mergers, and executive pay. In another intervention, the Federal Reserve has guaranteed more than $2 trillion in shaky short-term business loans and mortgages—and will purchase or guarantee an additional $1 trillion in 2009. Meanwhile the

Federal Deposit Insurance Corporation (FDIC), which guarantees bank checking deposits in the event of bank failures, has vastly increased the scope of its coverage, from $100,000 to $250,000 per bank account—and now also insures trillions of dollars in bank bonds and money market mutual funds, a gargantuan liability that it had never assumed before 2008. The FDIC now guarantees about 70 percent of all bank checking deposits, up from 50 percent a decade ago.

Such bailouts and government guarantees (and smaller bailouts targeted at large but insolvent insurance firms and money-losing Detroit automakers) resulted in an *$8.7 trillion* increase in federal obligations (debts and guarantees) in the second half of 2008 alone. To put this figure in perspective, consider that at the end of 2007 the entire national debt was $9.3 trillion, that annual spending in 2007 was $3 trillion, and that the country's entire annual economic output (GDP) in 2007 was $14 trillion. To compare the magnitude of recent interventions with those of the past, consider that the increase in spending in 2008–2009 is *seventeen times* the entire cost of FDR's [President Franklin D. Roosevelt's] New Deal (which was $500 billion, inflation-adjusted). And President Obama's first budget expands Washington's presence even further, with planned total spending of $4 trillion in 2009 (33 percent greater than in 2008), representing 28 percent of GDP (up from a 21-percent share in 2008).

Claims about the need to contain the supposed "instabilities" inherent in free markets have necessarily brought persistent demands that Washington regulate, bail out, guarantee, and nationalize financial institutions. According to the *Economist*, "the government of the world's leading capitalist nation has been sucked into the maelstrom of its most capitalist industry." This account blithely presumes that America today is a capitalist nation and that Washington politicians are victims of a capitalist marketplace, forced to intervene and fix the U.S, economy in the wake of its failures. Capitalism's modern critics presume that markets left to their own devices are inherently fragile and prone to breakdowns, whereas the U.S. government is a solid, confidence-instilling Rock of Gibraltar.

The current financial crisis was caused not by a return to free markets or pro-capitalist policies in the past decade, but by a tragic progression toward socialism.

Capitalism Is Innocent

The above interpretations ignore the plain fact that America today does not enjoy a free-market system—let alone a free-market financial sector—nor has it enjoyed one for most of the past century. Only through a profound misunderstanding of what constitutes a free-market system could anyone honestly blame capitalism for the financial crisis. For decades the American politico-economic system has been a *mixed* system—a combination of some freedom of choice and action offset by large (and growing) coercive interventions. It was precisely these coercive elements—the regulation, taxation, and subsidization—that caused today's financial crisis. Washington's recent and massive interventions did not follow from free-market "failure"; they followed from the market distortions caused by prior government intervention in the economy. Government interventions have both *instigated* and *aggravated* the latest financial crisis.

By surveying the government interventions that caused the latest turmoil and wealth destruction in housing and banking, this article will demonstrate that the current financial crisis was caused not by a return to free markets or pro-capitalist policies in the past decade, but by a tragic progression toward socialism. More importantly, it will demonstrate that altruism—the notion that being moral consists in sacrificing oneself for the needs of others—is the basis for this government intervention, and thus the root cause of the crisis.

Of course, in order to recognize that capitalism is innocent of the latest charges against it, we must bear in mind what capitalism is. Capitalism is the social system of individual rights, including property rights, in which all property is privately owned. Capitalism upholds the rule of law and equality before the law, forbids government favors to any person or group (including businesses), entails the *complete* separation of state and economics, and thus leaves each individual free to act on his own judgment for his own sake. With that in mind, let us consider the relevant facts surrounding the financial crisis.

The Troubled Housing Market

Perhaps no single U.S. government intervention has destroyed more capital or wasted more taxpayer funds in recent years than the establishment of "Fannie Mae," "Freddie Mac," and "Ginnie Mae"—"government-sponsored enterprises" (GSEs) that for years have been used by politicians to secure campaign funds and votes by promoting artificially cheap home mortgages and "the American dream of home ownership." The quaint, disarming nicknames for the GSEs actually stand for the Federal National Mortgage Association, the Federal Home Loan Mortgage Corporation, and the Government National Mortgage Association.

It is simply ludicrous for anyone today to speak of the U.S. mortgage sector as having been a fully "free" market before the latest crisis.

Until their recent insolvencies, the GSEs were neither wholly private firms nor wholly government agencies, but "hybrid" entities, with origins in FDR's New Deal. The GSEs were established to make home mortgages more available to the "needy," and for decades had the implicit backing of the U.S. Treasury and immunity from strict accounting standards, so as to reduce interest costs and dilute eligibility rules. Beginning in the mid-1990s, the influence of the GSEs was expanded significantly. The altruistic motive behind the expansion, embraced by Democrats and Republicans alike, was to help the needy and undeserving obtain mortgages they would not be able to secure in an unsubsidized, unregulated market.

Given the broad scope of government intervention in the U.S. home mortgage sector through the GSEs, the maze of other agencies—such as the Department of Housing and Urban Development (HUD), the Federal Housing Finance Board (FHFB), the Federal Housing Administration (FHA), the Federal Home Loan Bank (FHLB), and the Office of Federal Housing Enterprise Oversight (OFHEO)—and the cascade of Congressional acts—such as the Fair Housing Act (1968), the Equal Credit Opportunity Act (1974), the Community Reinvestment Act (1977), the Home Mortgage Disclosure Act (1975), the National Affordable Housing Act (1990), the Community Development and Regulatory Improvement Act (1994), the Home Ownership and Equity Protection Act (1994), and the American Dream Down Payment Act (2003)—it is simply ludicrous for anyone today to speak of the U.S. mortgage sector as having been a fully "free" market before the latest crisis. Only more ludicrous is the claim that the few free elements still remaining, but not the interventions, caused the crisis. Armed with its allegedly "noble" goal of increasing home ownership for the needy, the U.S. government has riddled the mortgage market with perverse incentives and unjust interventions that either compel or induce banks to lend to less-than-creditworthy borrowers, and thus to put themselves at greater risk of insolvency.

The Hazard Posed by Altruism

Today the concept of "moral hazard"—whereby a public policy necessarily engenders risky and reckless behavior by people and companies that otherwise simply would not arise (or not arise systemically) in a free market—is nearly ubiquitous. Some people now sense what economists (who coined the phrase) have long argued, that Washington's interventions in home mortgages have created such a "moral hazard" and thus contributed to the crisis. Yet few dare to name the real moral hazard at the root of all the recklessness: the hazard posed by the morality of altruism.

Altruism has motivated the utter debasement of lending standards in the past decade. Mortgage lenders joked that the Bush administration's crazed push to increase home ownership among blacks and Hispanics led to a proliferation of so-called "NINJA" loans—those granted to borrowers with "No Income, No Job, or Assets." Altruism commands service to the needy—and NINJA "borrowers" fit the bill perfectly. Highlighting the legal-coercive backing of Washington's altruistic credit policies, the Federal Reserve Bank has for years distributed a booklet to mortgage lenders—*Closing the Gap: A Guide to Equal Opportunity Lending*—which includes sidebar reminders that fines and jail terms await those found to be deficient in fighting "discrimination" by lending to the less-than-creditworthy. The booklet, still distributed today, derides as "arbitrary and unreasonable" such traditional credit standards as a 20 percent down payment (or loan-to-value ratio of 80 percent), an above-par credit score, a history of paying one's bills on time, and a steady job yielding an income sufficient to make monthly mortgage payments.

In order to "close the gap" and "achieve the American dream," "subprime" mortgages were extended to those with poor credit histories and those who put down little or no equity, leaving neither a collateral cushion for lenders nor an incentive for borrowers to repay their loans if house prices declined below the loan value. "Fannie Mae" and "Freddie Mac" further encouraged the expansion of subprime mortgage loans by encouraging loan originators to package them into instruments called "mortgage-backed securities" for sale either directly to the taxpayer-backed GSEs or to private investors with a GSE guarantee—a process known as "securitization." The GSEs then pressured rating agencies such as Moody's and Standard & Poor's to assign top grades to these low-grade securities in order to entice financial institutions throughout the world to purchase them. Because banks and mortgage firms were encouraged by the GSEs to sell their home mortgages shortly after originating them—in the process collecting rich fees and then jettisoning the consequences of borrowers defaulting on their loans—they became far less concerned about the quality of their borrowers or their loans.

Few dare to name the real moral hazard at the root of all the recklessness: the hazard posed by the morality of altruism.

Government's Altruistic Goal

The incentive to lend (or borrow) with care in the mortgage sector was radically diminished when, in 2002, Washington set a goal of artificially boosting the home ownership rate from 65 percent of households (the rate for the prior two decades) to 70 percent. Washington's array of mortgage agencies and laws were deployed to meet the altruistic goal, which necessitated the lowering of credit standards. Banks subject to the Community Reinvestment Act were aggressively penalized if they were not found boosting their subprime loan volumes; and to deprive them of any excuse, the GSEs began significantly increasing their purchases and guarantees of such loans.

Washington's overt sponsorship of debased lending standards in home loans was the primary economic cause of America's 2007–2009 mortgage-housing crisis. Washington provided massive political-financial incentives to make bad loans. Such loans were made, and soon exhibited sky-high default rates. High default rates caused bank losses, so bankers restricted their lending, resulting in a peak (and decline) in

167

house prices that wiped out home equity and caused further defaults. The highest default rates on subprime mortgages have occurred in such immigrant-heavy states as Arizona, California, and Florida, where, through altruistic schemes, politicians expected to generate a wave of new voters. . . .

Paying for Altruism

It should surprise no one that the altruism-infested "credit market" has been impractical—and impractical even as regards the altruistic goal of helping the needy to own homes. Washington pushed to raise the national home ownership rate from 65 percent to 70 percent and to narrow the "gap" in ownership rates between white and nonwhite households, but in the wake of that push—as mortgage defaults and home foreclosures skyrocketed—the home ownership rate, after rising a bit, is now slipping *below* 65 percent, while the "gap," having narrowed in years before 2002, has been widening since 2007. Home ownership rates among blacks and Hispanics, those who were targeted by the Bush administration, have dropped precipitously, in many cases to *below* the prior peaks that were deemed unsatisfactory by the social planners.

America's financial market is suffering not because of greed or freedom, but because of the widespread acceptance of altruism and the consequent government intervention in banking.

Who is to foot the gargantuan bill for this altruism-induced mess? Just as altruism would have it: the *innocent*—the innocent taxpayers and the 93 percent of all American home owners who pay their mortgages on time but now will be forced to pay other people's mortgages and to bail out businesses they did not botch and do not own. . . .

Altruism Should Be Rejected

Acceptance of altruism leads people to abandon their self-interest, the profit motive, the basic principles of economics, and the basic principle of America: the principle of individual rights. But these values are essential to good living, to wealth creation, to a healthy economy, and to a just society. America's financial market is suffering not because of greed or freedom, but because of the widespread acceptance of altruism and the consequent government intervention in banking.

The financial crisis is, fundamentally, a *moral* crisis. The extent to which Americans accept that they have a moral duty to sacrifice for the sake of others is the extent to which they will allow our government to compel us all to do so—by means of further interventions, further subsidies, further controls. To end the crisis, we must acknowledge that government intervention caused it, and we must demand that the government begin removing its coercive hands from the economy. With an eye to the short term, we must demand that it scale back the powers of the GSEs, the Federal Reserve, and the FDIC; and with an eye to the long term, we must demand that the government abolish these agencies entirely and restore a gold standard run by private, currency-issuing banks subject solely to the objective commercial and bankruptcy codes. But in order to advocate these reforms, Americans must reject the moral code that stands in the way. We must reject altruism. We must defend each individual's right to exist, not as a slave to the needs of others, but for his own sake—bankers included.

Government Intervention Caused the Global Financial Crisis

Yaron Brook and Don Watkins

Yaron Brook is the president of the Ayn Rand Center for Individual Rights, a division of the Ayn Rand Institute, and Don Watkins is a writer at the Ayn Rand Center for Individual Rights.

Speaking of the financial crisis, French president Nicolas Sarkozy recently [2008] said, "Laissez-faire is finished. The all-powerful market that always knows best is finished."

It Is Not Capitalism

Sarkozy was echoing the views of many, including president-elect [Barack] Obama, who assume that the financial crisis was caused by free markets—by "unbridled greed" unleashed by decades of deregulation and a "hands off" approach to the economy. And given this premise, the solution, they say, is obvious. To solve this crisis and prevent another one, we need a heavy dose of Uncle Sam's elixir: government intervention. Whether it's more bailouts, stricter regulation, a new round of nationalizations, or some other scheme, the only question since day one has been *how*, not *whether*, government is going to intervene.

And the issue is wider than the financial crisis. Millions of Americans don't have health insurance? Well, says Obama, that's because we've left the health-care system to the free market. The solution: a complete government takeover of medicine. A few companies engaged in accounting fraud? It must be because we didn't impose enough regulations on businessmen. The solution: rein in corporations with Sarbanes-Oxley [legislation for corporations that defines which business records need to be saved and for how long].

But while capitalism may be a convenient scapegoat, it did not cause any of these problems. Indeed, whatever one wishes to call the unruly mixture of freedom and government controls that made up our economic and political system during the last three decades, one cannot call it capitalism.

Intervention Is Inconsistent with Capitalism

Take a step back. In the lead up to the "Reagan Revolution," the explosive growth of government during the '60s and '70s had left the American economy in disarray. A crushing tax burden, runaway inflation, brutal unemployment, and economic stagnation had Americans looking for an alternative. That's what [Ronald] Reagan offered, denouncing big government and promising a new "morning in America."

Under Reagan, some taxes were reduced, inflation was subdued, a few regulations were relaxed—and the economy roared back to life. But while markets were able to function to a greater degree than in the immediate past, the regulatory and welfare state remained largely untouched, with government spending continuing to increase, as well as some taxes. Later administrations were even worse. [George W.] Bush . . . , often laughably called a champion of free markets, presided over massive new governmental controls like Sarbanes-Oxley and massive new welfare programs like the prescription drug benefit.

None of this is consistent with capitalism. As the economic system that fully recognizes and protects individual rights, including the right to private property, capitalism means, in Ayn Rand's words, "the abolition of any and all forms of government intervention in production and trade, the separation of State and Economics, in the same way and for the same reasons as the separation of Church and State."

Laissez-faire means laissez-faire: no welfare state entitlements, no Federal Reserve monetary manipulation, no regulatory bullying, no controls, no government interference in the economy. The government's job under capitalism is single but crucial: to protect individual rights from violation by force or fraud.

America came closest to this system in the latter half of the nineteenth century. The result was an unprecedented explosion of wealth creation and consequent rise in the standard of living. Even now, when the fading remnants of capitalism are badly crippled by endless controls, we see that the freest countries—those which retain the most capitalist elements—have the highest standard of living.

Capitalism is blamed for the ills of government intervention—and then even more government intervention is proposed as the cure.

A Pattern of Blaming Capitalism

Why then should capitalism take the blame today—when capitalism doesn't even exist? Consider the current crisis. The causes are complex, but the driving force is clearly government intervention: the Fed [Federal Reserve] keeping interest rates below the rate of inflation, thus encouraging people to borrow and providing the impetus for a housing bubble; the Community Reinvestment Act, which forces banks to lend money to low-income and poor-credit households; the creation of Fannie Mae [Federal National Mortgage Association] and Freddie Mac [Federal Home Loan Mortgage Corporation] with government-guaranteed debt leading to artificially low mortgage rates and the illusion that the financial instruments created by bundling them are low risk; government-licensed rating agencies, which gave AAA ratings to mortgage-backed securities, creating a false sense of confidence; deposit insurance and the "too big to fail" doctrine, whose bailout promises have created huge distortions in incentives and risk-taking throughout the financial system; and so on. In the face of this long list, who can say with a straight face that the housing and financial markets were frontiers of "cowboy capitalism"?

This is just the latest example of a pattern that has been going on since the rise of capitalism: capitalism is blamed for the ills of government intervention—and then even more government intervention is proposed as the cure. The Great Depression? Despite massive evidence that the Federal Reserve's and other government policies were responsible for the crash and the inability of the economy to recover, it was laissez-faire that was blamed. Consequently, in the aftermath, the government's power over the economy was not curtailed but dramatically expanded. Or what about the energy crisis of the 1970s? Despite compelling evidence that it was brought on by monetary inflation exacerbated by the abandonment of the remnants of the gold standard, and made worse by prices controls, "greedy" oil companies were blamed. The prescribed "solution" was for the government to exert even more control.

It's time to stop blaming capitalism for the sins of government intervention, and give true laissez-faire a chance. Now that would be a change we could believe in.

CHAPTER 4

Does the Public Good Warrant Government Intervention in Capitalism?

Chapter Preface

One of the defining features of capitalism is the private ownership of wealth. Under capitalism, individuals or corporations own resources, land, and information used for the further production of wealth and profit. Individuals, then, are free to go into business where they see the demand for a product or service. This is in contrast to other economic systems, such as socialism, where the means of production are owned publicly and managed by the government. Government ownership of certain entities, however, often exists alongside a general adoption of capitalism in other areas.

There are many examples around the world where government owns and manages businesses central to the public good. For example, government ownership of transportation infrastructure is common because of the centrality of transportation to the public good. The U.S. passenger train system—Amtrak—is a government-owned corporation, despite the fact that the American economic system is largely capitalist. In many countries, even airlines are owned by the government—some examples include Air New Zealand, Air Malawi, Iraqi Airways, and Vietnam Airlines. The airlines in America, however, such as American Airlines and Southwest Airlines, are corporations owned by their stockholders.

Beyond the government ownership of business, governments frequently own property seen as central to the public good. In America, this includes national and state parks; property used by public entities such as schools, post offices, and emergency services; and property necessary for roads. In addition, the U.S. government reserves the right to exercise eminent domain, meaning that the government may forcefully take private property—though with compensation—for the use of public needs such as highways. Eminent domain is particularly worrisome to many proponents of capitalism, as journalist and author John Stossel has argued in *Capitalism Magazine*, because it undermines the amount of security private property owners can have.

Another example of the American government providing a service that could be provided by for-profit business is the U.S. Postal Service. The U.S. Postal Service has a monopoly on the delivery of non-urgent letters in the United States. Two large corporations, FedEx and United Parcel Service (UPS), offer competition for express mail and packages, but they are not permitted to use mailboxes designed for use by the U.S. Postal Service at residential and commercial locations. Government-run postal service in America has been in existence since 1775, justified by the Postal Clause in the U.S. Constitution, which allows Congress "to establish post offices and post roads." The system allows for the same price rates for customers, whether they live in dense, urban areas or in rural areas. Many capitalists see this as a distortion of the true cost of mail and they argue for privatization. Rick Geddes, associate professor in the Department of Policy Analysis and Management at Cornell University, has argued in the *Hoover Digest* that private businesses should be allowed to compete with the U.S. Postal Service for all kinds of mail delivered.

Even in largely capitalistic economies such as that of the United States, government intervention occurs, especially when such intervention is seen as promoting the public good. There is widespread disagreement, however, about whether government intervention is ever justified and, if so, under what circumstances.

Government Intervention in Health Care Is Preferable

Ian Williams

Ian Williams is a writer and speaker. He is the author of Deserter: George Bush's War on Military Families, Veterans, and His Past.

Some years ago in New York I went to hear the Taiwanese health minister describe the country's new National Health Service. He had just been to visit George W. Bush's first secretary of health, Tommy Thompson. I could not resist and asked, "While you were in Washington, did you explain to the Republican secretary of health that you've introduced a socialized health system?" He looked me squarely in the eyes and said, "You know, it completely slipped my mind!" And well it might. We have heard much tendentious information about the alleged success of Chile's privatization of social security, but little of the unchallenged efficacy of Taiwan's health service.

Taiwan's Health Insurance Program

Taiwan inaugurated its National Health Insurance [NHI] program in 1995. Before then the three major social health insurance programs, Labor Insurance, Government Employee Insurance, and Farmers Insurance, left 40 percent of the population uncovered, many of them children and retirees. Dr. Michael Chen, vice president and chief financial officer of the NHI Bureau, says that there is now 99 percent coverage—he is not sure who the missing 1 percent are, but suspects that they are expatriates who have not registered (apparently, prison inmates are not covered but do receive

Ian Williams, "Health Care in Taiwan: Why Can't the United States Learn Some Lessons?" *Dissent*, vol. 55, no. 1, Winter 2008, pp. 12–17. Copyright © 2008 by Dissent Publishing Corporation. Reproduced by permission of the University of Pennsylvania Press.

care in the prison system). Indeed, many expatriates maintain their coverage—including the million or so who now work in mainland China. Conversely, foreign workers in Taiwan are also covered.

NHI premiums cover Western- and Chinese-style medicine, both in- and outpatient, prescription charges, home care, and dentistry. Almost all western-style hospitals and 88 percent of Chinese-medicine clinics are in the system. Though dentists have been opting out of the British National Health dental system in large numbers, almost 95 percent of dental clinics are in the Taiwanese system. Health care is provided by a competitive mixture of municipal and public (about one-third of the beds) and privately owned hospitals that also offer comprehensive primary care. Between them they employ almost two-thirds of doctors. Avoiding the severe conflict of interest that the British system has maintained, doctors contracted to hospitals cannot run private practices on the side.

A Single Payer Scheme

Taiwan is a smaller (twenty-one million people), more compact country than the United States, but the NHI provides many pointers for Americans attempting to secure full health coverage. To begin with, Taiwan had a vigorous market-based health provision system, which has adapted itself, apparently very happily, to the new national service. The former Kuo-Mintang [KMT] government was an authoritarian social democracy, in the very limited sense that social provision was on the agenda. But corruption and capitalism were fully developed. The NHI was introduced in the early days of democracy, just as the KMT single-party system was being dismantled. It was a popular election issue.

The provision of health care is not nationalized, despite a degree of information and coordination that, for example, the British system cannot match after spending billions on computerization. Rather, the NHI is a classic single payer scheme—the government runs a compulsory, mostly premium-financed insurance system, which negotiates a single payment schedule with the private and municipal or government-owned providers.

In 2003, health spending per head in Taiwan was less than $800 per head of population compared to the U.S. level of approximately $5,500.

On the face of it, the experience of the insured in Taiwan is certainly better than that of Americans dependent on the caprices of commercial health insurers. In 2005, polls showed a 72.5 percent satisfaction rate—and much of the dissatisfaction is with the cost, laughably small though it is by U.S. standards. When co-payments and premiums were increased in 2002, the satisfaction rate plummeted to 59.7 percent. To put this in perspective, the premiums at the maximum are less than $20 (U.S.) per month (the annual per capita GDP [gross domestic product] is $16,500 U.S.).

Taiwan has done this for proportionately less than half the cost of the United States, with costs running at 6.2 percent of gross domestic product in 2005, compared with the following for other countries: United States, 15.2 percent; France, 10.1 percent; Canada, 9.9 percent; United Kingdom, 7.7 percent; Japan, 7.9 percent; South Korea, 5.2 percent (World Health Organization figures for 2003 published in 2006).

In absolute terms, the difference is even starker. In 2003, health spending per head in Taiwan was less than $800 per head of population compared to the U.S. level of approximately $5,500. In fact, by 2005, U.S. health care spending increased 6.9 percent to almost $2.0 trillion, or $6,697 per person, amounting to 16 percent of GDP.

Contained Costs with Choice

With an aging population demanding more and more innovative medical interventions, the NHI faces similar problems to the United States in terms of the escalation of demand (and thus of cost), but it has contained the growth of health care costs as a share of GDP while expanding coverage to a far higher proportion of hitherto uninsured people than in the United States.

Unlike health maintenance organizations in the United States, there are simply no waiting lists, except perhaps for organ donor availability.

The various constituencies seem to have cooperated to avert long-term financial problems, adjusting premiums, co-payments, and provider fees in a way that has left them all reasonably content, while providing protection for weaker and poorer groups and those suffering chronic illnesses. Even the generous safety net seems to have another net below, with exemptions for those who cannot pay, loan option to pay premiums, and referral to charitable organizations for payment when even that fails. For example, by the end of 2004, the NHI had issued 750,000 "Catastrophic Illness" cards, whose holders' co-payments are either reduced or eliminated entirely. This makes sound social but bad financial sense, as these people account for almost a quarter of the bureau's expenditure—but that is what national insurance is about.

A common argument against "socialized medicine" in the United States is that it leads to rationing and waiting lists for treatment. However, unlike the Canadian or British systems, and, indeed, unlike health maintenance organizations [HMOs] in the United States, there are simply no waiting lists, except perhaps for organ donor availability. That is in part because, although there is a government sponsored single-payer system, there is not a single provider, and the insured have free choice of doctors and institutions. Indeed, Deputy Minister of Health Tsay Jinn Chen refers to "doctor shopping" on the part of the insured, which introduces market discipline and ensures speedy treatment.

Transition Problems

Of course, the system did not start running as designed immediately. It has needed adjustment, not least to balance revenue and costs and manage demand in a way that does not impinge on health care. In fact, the system does seem to have a considerable degree of adaptability.

When the British National Health System was established in 1947, there were two major fiscal problems. One was that, as Health Minister Aneurin Bevan said, he had to "stuff the maws of doctors with gold" to get them into the system. That was in part because the government was, in effect, nationalizing the old hospitals and employing the doctors on a contractual basis. The other problem, which would be relevant for any U.S. introduction of national insurance, was the "overhang," the pent-up demand for dentistry, prescription medicine, dentures, and glasses from millions of previously uncovered patients. In Taiwan, Chen described the new system as something like "an all-you-can-eat" restaurant for very hungry people, who no longer had to trade off other purchases against health care.

The introduction of co-payments in Britain in the early 1950s, as a result of the costs of the Korean War, occasioned a huge ideological battle in the Labour Party, with Harold Wilson, later the prime minister, leading a revolt on behalf of a completely free service. In retrospect, admirable though the motives of the Labour revolt may have been, Taiwan's program of nominal co-payments, with suitable provision for the genuinely needy, seems a sensible way to manage and filter demand.

Containing Costs

In order to contain costs, in 2005 the NHI introduced a referral system, aimed at dissuading the insured from racing to the most prestigious hospital or specialist with every headache. They can still do that, but now they face an increased co-payment if they skip referral. The co-payments should not dissuade anyone genuinely ill from seeking help—it is a mere $12 U.S. for an unreferred patient who chooses to go to an Academic Medical Center. For those who go first to a clinic, referred or unreferred, the co-payment is $1.50 U.S.

For some expensive high-tech and experimental procedures preauthorization is needed, but it would appear that this is less onerous than dealing with an American HMO. Equitably counterbalancing the co-payments are ceilings on in-treatment liabilities—for example, an annual cumulative ceiling of approximately $1,300 or 10 percent of per capita income for co-payments. The ceiling has a safety net hanging from it as well, with many exceptions for serious illness, childbirth, rural and outlying areas, and low-income families, to ensure that no one is deterred from seeking the help they need.

Prescription costs are managed similarly. First, the NHI bargains down drug prices and second, co-payments are on a proportional scale with a ceiling of approximately $6. Once again, there are many exemptions for the needy.

Health Care Delivery *important.*

The NHI benefits from a longstanding public health system that, even under the KuoMintang, provided a network of inoculation and vaccination, children's and women's health care, and which had reduced or eliminated the diseases that otherwise would be prevalent in a subtropical developing country. The NHI is proud, for example, of its 95 percent inoculation rate against measles, which compares to 70 percent in Japan.

Although the competitive free market in health was probably an important factor in averting waiting lists, it did have other consequences, one of which, as [public health policy professors] Jui-Fen Rachel Lu and William C. Hsiao charge, is that "Taiwan has a fragmented health care delivery system that lacks continuity of care. Its clinical quality of care suffers from years of laissez-faire policy toward clinical practices." There are, however, more and more quality controls. By law, only licensed doctors can own a hospital or clinic, for example. Building on that, the persuasive power of the NHI has been creating a family doctor system, in which between five to ten primary care clinics in each area are networked with NHI contracted hospitals to provide an integrated care system, with referrals when needed but with primary care continuity.

The NHI Card

It seems that the family practice is an innovation for Taiwan, but harnessed to the network, and with the detailed record keeping made possible by the NHI card, it ensures better primary care. A smart chip in the new insurance cards allows the NHI to look for examples of fraud, overbilling, and similar practices that bedevil Medicare. There are significant fringe benefits, too, for example, keeping track of organ donors, which is especially important in a society where donation is not that common.

NHI providers use the card for financial purposes but also increasingly for clinical record keeping. Since 2004, the IC card has given users access to details of serious illness and injury and major medical examinations and scans, avoiding unnecessary and expensive repeat tests of the kind that happen so frequently in the United States. It stores records of both prescriptions and drug allergies, thus averting the problems of adverse interactions between different medicines, and duplication of prescriptions for dangerous or expensive drugs. In previous years the system was prone to overprescribing and prescription inflation, but the card checked that tendency. One of the most valuable applications of the NHI's information system is that of tracking down suspected cases and heading off an epidemic disease, as in the case of SARS [severe acute respiratory syndrome].

The card makes it much easier to monitor and detect fraud. In 2004, the NHI reduced or deducted claims from over a thousand institutions, 231 were awarded demerits, which affect their contract payment levels, and 90 were suspended from the system for periods of one to three months. Four were dropped entirely. The information system is so effective that a former CEO of the NHI Bureau once quipped that he knew immediately if the same tooth had "been pulled twice" from any individual.

Revenue and Costs

The IC card helps track payment of premiums and allows prompt reminders of missed premium payments, which ensures coverage for the insured and, equally vital, cash flow for the system. Since it was set up, the costs of the NHI have risen by an annual average of 5.5 percent, while revenues have only risen by 4.7 percent, hence the need for constant fine-tuning of co-payments and attempts to restrain expenditures, which are currently between $11 and $12 billion U.S. The fund is mandated to carry a one-month buffer but has rarely been able to do so. Solutions have included doubling the tobacco tax surcharge and raising the earnings ceiling on contributions, which currently stands at a little over $4,000 per month.

Premium collection is similar to that of Social Security contributions in the United States. Employers and the self-employed are legally bound to pay. However, unlike the US Social Security Fund, the NHI is a genuine pay-as-you go system. The aim is for the premium income to pay costs.

There is a continual tussle over who bears the cost of the national service—currently 27 percent is paid by the government, 35 percent by employers, and 38 percent by employees. The various partners try to shift the burden, and legislators are reluctant to incur popular displeasure by increasing costs to employees, while the influential employers' organizations also have the ear of negotiators. They talked down the employers' share of the premium from 80 percent to 60 percent. The government puts in another 10 percent.

The government share, including the tobacco tax surcharge and lottery proceeds, goes disproportionately—but appropriately—to finance the premiums of disadvantaged groups, remote rural dwellers, the indigenous peoples, and the poor. Although all contributors have access to the same services, there is a significant redistributive effect. Six categories of insured pay at different levels, scaled against income, with ceilings.

The single-payer system means that the NHI is a monopoly purchaser and so has greater bargaining power with the pharmaceutical companies and with the providers.

The insured pay for each dependent, up to a ceiling of three, while the employers pay for an average number of dependents, which takes away the incentive to fire or not hire fecund workers. For the "regional population," in remote rural areas, the government pays 40 percent and the insured pays 60 percent of the premium, while for low-income households, the government pays the whole premium.

Monopoly Power

The single-payer system means that the NHI is a monopoly purchaser and so has greater bargaining power with the pharmaceutical companies and with the providers. As in Canada and the United Kingdom, the pharmaceutical companies have to accept reasonable prices, because the NHI has a weight in prescription pricing that is deliberately denied Medicare in the latest U.S. Medicare prescription plan.

Facing up to the pharmaceutical industry allows the single-payer system to control costs, and the technology of the NHI card allows controls of overcharging. It even encourages best

practices, such as appropriate use of antibiotics for upper respiratory chest infections, or antacids for stomach problems.
The twenty-nine million monthly claims going through the
system allow effective analysis of costs and billing patterns.

The NHI does not seem to have abused its monopoly
power to drive down doctors' earnings, as there is vigorous
competition among practitioners and institutions for patient
patronage, even at the fees collectively agreed upon. The ease
of payment, with the government writing the checks, seems to
have been a good enough trade-off for the doctors. There is
nothing to stop a doctor setting up private practice—except a
shortage of clients. The system was originally based on fee for
service but then transitioned to a "case-payment" system based
on fifty-three items. The program's chief financial officer,
Michael Chen, says that the idea is that the NHI is purchasing
"not just medical care, but health, as evidenced by initiatives
aiming at encouraging 'pay for performance.'" The 95 percent
inoculation rate against measles suggests the success of the
program.

---

*Many features of the Taiwanese system lend themselves
readily to the United States.*

The NHI Committee for the Arbitration of Medical Costs
considers not only the overall figures but also individual
providers' performance based on support for patients' rights,
accessibility and satisfaction, efficiency of service, and similar
criteria. The committee rewards providers if scored for "excel-
lence" through the "quality assurance funds."

The United States

When General Motors offloads its health care system onto the
United Auto Workers, one suspects that disaster has been
postponed rather than averted. The Taiwanese example of the
single-payer system should prove attractive to everybody but

executives and shareholders of health insurers. Many features of the Taiwanese system lend themselves readily to the United States, which is not surprising, because, as Chen admits, the primary model for it was Medicare. But the adjustments the Taiwanese made point to the road not taken in the United States. Avoiding the commercial health insurers for a single-payer system with universal coverage offers great efficiencies at almost every point of the provision network.

The Taiwanese system begins with an idealistic premise—of universal, high-quality health coverage—but then addresses in a most pragmatic way the actual behavior of the constituencies involved: the medical providers, the pharmaceutical companies, and the patients. The frequent readjustments do not pander to the moral panic of freeloading or fraud that often governs legislation and decision-making in the United Kingdom and the United States, but rather to actual, observable behavior.

Of course, the U.S. federal system offers an obstacle to any outright imitation, but no more so than the Canadian provincial system, and, as so often, states could be convinced to participate easily by offering, for example, a proportion of the tobacco taxes on a use-it-or-lose-it basis. Imagine the possibilities if the $250 billion U.S. global tobacco settlement had been allocated to a health insurance scheme instead of, in effect, providing walking around money for the states party to the settlement.

Isn't it strange that Taiwan, so long dear to the hearts of anticommunist conservatives in the United States, should produce such a socially innovative model? But maybe the source of the model will overcome some of their reflexive opposition.

Social Security Should Be Run by the Government

Institute for America's Future

The Institute for America's Future is a non-partisan research and education center that develops policy ideas, educational materials, and outreach programs to help shape a progressive agenda.

Social Security is back in the news. In a town-hall event on July 7, 2008, a young woman asked Arizona Senator [and 2008 presidential candidate] John McCain if she was likely to receive Social Security benefits someday. In his reply, McCain lamented Social Security's design and structure and, as he had elsewhere, indicated that he would radically change this successful program. He said, "Americans have got to understand that we are paying present-day retirees with the taxes paid by young workers in America today, and that's a disgrace, it's an absolute disgrace and it's got to be fixed."

We've been here before. Three years ago [2005], President [George W.] Bush declared that Social Security faced a financial crisis, and his solution was privatization—taking payroll taxes we all pay into the system and investing a portion of those funds in private stock market accounts. Now John McCain is bringing the idea back. In March 2008, McCain told the *Wall Street Journal*, "As part of Social Security reform, I believe that private savings accounts are a part of it—along the lines that President Bush proposed." The idea became more concrete in July 2008, when McCain named economist Martin Feldstein, the "chief intellectual force behind privatization," as a surrogate on his campaign. These moves revive an idea that the American people rejected three years ago.

Institute for America's Future, *The Perils of Privatization: Social Security Privatization Cuts Lifetime Benefits; Makes Senior Citizens Vulnerable to Poverty: The Impact in the United States*. Washington, D.C.: Institute for America's Future, 2008. Reproduced by permission.

This report updates research published by the Institute for America's Future at that time. It estimates the reduction in Social Security benefits that a typical United States resident can expect and the number of seniors exposed to poverty if Social Security were privatized. The main findings are that:

In the United States, Social Security privatization:

- Cuts life-time benefits by $240,264

- Makes 8.6 million senior citizens vulnerable to poverty.

Social Security Works

Social Security is not a "disgrace." It is a successful social program and a profound intergenerational promise. Every generation pays into Social Security during its turn, and withdraws from Social Security when its time comes. Social Security has been successfully operating that way for over 70 years.

Social Security works. It lifts 1.3 million children and nearly 13 million senior citizens out of poverty. Social Security provides 73 percent of the typical retiree's income, compared to 17 percent from pensions and 10 percent from savings and other sources.

Every generation pays into Social Security during its turn, and withdraws from Social Security when its time comes.

Before Social Security, nearly half of American seniors lived in poverty. Today, fewer than 9 percent of seniors spend their "golden years" in poverty. Social Security is especially important now, with private sector pensions disappearing and savings scarce. According to the estimates by the Economic Policy Institute, without Social Security, more than 35 percent of Americans aged 65 and older would be living in poverty.

A False Crisis

Some politicians and conservative privatization advocates have created a myth that Social Security is in crisis. They issue dire warnings and predict imminent bankruptcy. McCain told the young woman in the July town hall event that it was "unlikely" she would receive her benefits. President Bush tells a story of a poll of young people who "think it's more likely they're going to see a UFO than get a Social Security check." The White House web site elaborates: "If we do not act to fix Social Security now, the only solutions will be dramatically higher taxes, massive new borrowing or sudden and severe cuts in Social Security benefits or other government programs."

The proclamations work. One poll says that 73 percent of Americans believe Social Security has "major problems" or is in "crisis."

The reality is far different. Social Security currently has a surplus of $2 trillion. The surplus is projected to increase to over $4 trillion by 2016, more than four times the amount needed to pay benefits in that year. According to cautious estimates by the Congressional Budget Office, the Social Security trust fund would not be depleted until 2046.

Privatization replaces the guaranteed floor of economic security with the uncertainty of the stock market.

The Problems of Privatization

Privatization means diverting deductions from the Social Security trust fund into private accounts run by private investment companies. Conservatives have touted privatization for years as a way to increase returns on investment. Privatization, however, has a variety of problems.

First, privatization would transfer huge administrative fees to Wall Street. Managing large numbers of small accounts is inherently inefficient. Administrative costs for private systems in Mexico, Chile and Argentina are between 1.8 to 2.4 percent of the program total; in England, administrative costs are 3.2 percent. In contrast, administrative costs of Social Security run less than one percent.

Second, diverting funds would cause the trust fund's surplus to run out much sooner, leading to benefit reductions and retirement insecurity—the opposite of Social Security's intergenerational promise. The Center on Budget and Policy Priorities estimates that President's Bush's plan would have created $17.7 trillion in additional debt by 2050.

Third, and most importantly, privatization replaces the guaranteed floor of economic security with the uncertainty of the stock market. In 2007, Social Security guaranteed economic security to more than 49 million grandparents, parents and children worldwide. Individuals are free, of course, to invest their personal savings in the stock market—but Social Security guarantees a floor beneath which their fortunes will not fall.

Current Social Security Data

In the United States, 48.5 million count on their earned Social Security benefit every month. In addition to the benefits that Social Security provides to United States families, it also provides a stable level of individual income that fuels the United States' economy. Thousands of businesses, and the state government, also depend on the Social Security guarantee. Fully $580.5 billion in individual income flows into the United States' economy from Social Security each year—roughly $48.4 billion every month.

Privatization would cast many seniors below the poverty line. According to the U.S. Census Bureau, the number of people from the United States living in poverty in 2006 was 36.5 million. In 2005, 15.5 million United States seniors relied on Social Security checks for at least half of their total income. 7.9 million of these individuals depend on these benefits for almost all—90 percent or more—of their total income. Today, the average Social Security check for individual retirees in the United States is $1,088 per month. But $867 per month is needed just to stay above the federal poverty line. These individuals are close to the edge, and vulnerable to swings in the cost of food, housing or energy.

Privatization and Benefit Cuts

The Center on Budget and Policy Priorities calculated in 2005 that if a Bush-style privatization plan were enacted, children born around the time the plan started would have their annual guaranteed benefits cut by 50 percent when they retire. If that were to happen to current-day senior citizens in the United States, people with incomes up to 191% of the current poverty line would no longer have a guarantee that they would avoid poverty. Social Security would have failed in its promise of security. 8.6 million senior citizens in the United States would be left behind.

Second, benefits would be reduced even among people not plunged into poverty. Under a Bush-like privatization plan, a person born today in the United States who retires at the current full retirement age of 67, would see a lifetime benefit cut of $240,264 in today's dollars. This is the benefit cut a United States resident would suffer even *after* accounting for earning an average 4.35 percent return on their private account investment.

Social Security is not going bankrupt. But we do need to pay attention to the impact the retirement of the baby-boom generation is having on the program. The solution is to strengthen the existing structures, not to reinvent them or privatize them. Currently, the Social Security payroll tax currently applies only to the first $102,000 a worker makes—any earnings above that are tax-free. One simple solution is to apply the tax to some or all earnings above $102,000. Lifting that cap is a fair and minor adjustment that could prevent any shortfall after 2046.

Government Intervention in Health Care Violates Rights

Leonard Peikoff

Leonard Peikoff is the founder of the Ayn Rand Institute and author of Objectivism: The Philosophy of Ayn Rand.

Most people who oppose socialized medicine do so on the grounds that it is moral and well-intentioned, but impractical; that is, it is a noble idea—which just somehow does not work. I do not agree that socialized medicine is moral and well-intentioned, but impractical. Of course, it *is* impractical—it does *not* work—but I hold that it is impractical *because* it is immoral. This is not a case of noble in theory but a failure in practice; it is a case of vicious in theory and *therefore* a disaster in practice. I want to focus on the moral issue at stake. So long as people believe that socialized medicine is a noble plan, there is no way to fight it. You cannot stop a noble plan—not if it really is noble. The only way you can defeat it is to unmask it—to show that it is the very opposite of noble. Then at least you have a fighting chance.

American Rights

What is morality in this context? The American concept of it is officially stated in the Declaration of Independence. It upholds man's unalienable, individual *rights*. The term "rights," note, is a moral (not just a political) term; it tells us that a certain course of behavior is right, sanctioned, proper, a prerogative to be respected by others, not interfered with—and that anyone who violates a man's rights is: wrong, morally wrong, unsanctioned, evil.

Now our only rights, the American viewpoint continues, are the rights to life, liberty, property, and the pursuit of hap-

Leonard Peikoff, "Health Care Is Not A Right," delivered under the auspices of Americans for Free Choice in Medicine at a Town Hall Meeting on Health Care, Costa Mesa, December 11, 1993. Reproduced by permission of the author.

piness. That's all. According to the Founding Fathers, we are not born with a right to a trip to Disneyland, or a meal at McDonald's, or a kidney dialysis (nor with the 18th-century equivalent of these things). We have certain specific rights—and only these.

Only Rights to Action

Why *only* these? Observe that all legitimate rights have one thing in common: they are rights to action, not to rewards from other people. The American rights impose no obligations on other people, merely the negative obligation to leave you alone. The system guarantees you the chance to work for what you want—not to be given it without effort by somebody else.

The right to life, for example, does not mean that your neighbors have to feed and clothe you; it means you have the right to earn your food and clothes yourself, if necessary by a hard struggle, and that no one can forcibly stop your struggle for these things or steal them from you if and when you have achieved them. In other words: you have the right to act, and to keep the results of your actions, the products you make, to keep them or to trade them with others, if you wish. But you have no right to the actions or products of others, except on terms to which they voluntarily agree.

To take one more example: the right to the pursuit of happiness is precisely that: the right to the *pursuit*—to a certain type of action on your part and its result—not to any guarantee that other people will make you happy or even try to do so. Otherwise, there would be no liberty in the country: if your mere desire for something, anything, imposes a duty on other people to satisfy you, then they have no choice in their lives, no say in what they do, they have no liberty, they cannot pursue *their* happiness. Your "right" to happiness at their expense means that they become rightless serfs, that is your slaves. Your right to *anything* at others expense means that they become rightless.

That is why the U.S. system defines rights as it does, strictly as the rights to action. This was the approach that made the U.S. the first truly free country in all world history—and, soon afterwards, as a result, the greatest country in history, the richest and the most powerful. It became the most powerful because its view of rights made it the most moral. It was the country of individualism and personal independence.

The newfangled rights wipe out any real rights—and turn the people who actually create the goods and services involved into servants of the state.

Newfangled Rights

Today, however, we are seeing the rise of principled *immorality* in this country. We are seeing a total abandonment by the intellectuals and the politicians of the moral principles on which the U.S. was founded. We are seeing the complete destruction of the concept of rights. The original American idea has been virtually wiped out, ignored as if it had never existed. The rule now is for politicians to ignore and violate men's actual rights, while arguing about a whole list of rights never dreamed of in this country's founding documents—rights which require no earning, no effort, no action at all on the part of the recipient.

You are entitled to something, the politicians say, simply because it exists and you want or need it—period. You are entitled to be given it by the government. Where does the government get it from? What does the government have to do to private citizens—to their individual rights—to their *real* rights—in order to carry out the promise of showering free services on the people?

The answers are obvious. The newfangled rights wipe out real rights—and turn the people who actually create the goods and services involved into servants of the state. The Russians tried this exact system for many decades. Unfortunately, we have not learned from their experience. Yet the meaning of socialism is clearly evident in any field at all—you don't need to think of health care as a special case; it is just as apparent if the government were to proclaim a universal right to food, or to a vacation, or to a haircut. I mean: a right in the new sense: not that you are free to earn these things by your own effort and trade, but that you have a moral claim to be given these things free of charge, with no action on your part, simply as handouts from a benevolent government.

An Analogy to Health Care

How would these alleged new rights be fulfilled? Take the simplest case: you are born with a moral right to hair care, let us say, provided by a loving government free of charge to all who want or need it. What would happen under such a moral theory?

Haircuts are free, like the air we breathe, so some people show up every day for an expensive new styling, the government pays out more and more, barbers revel in their huge new incomes, and the profession starts to grow ravenously, bald men start to come in droves for free hair implantations, a school of fancy, specialized eyebrow pluckers develops—it's all free, the government pays. The dishonest barbers are having a field day, of course—but so are the honest ones; they are working and spending like mad, trying to give every customer his heart's desire, which is a millionaire's worth of special hair care and services—the government starts to scream, the budget is out of control. Suddenly directives erupt: we must limit the number of barbers, we must limit the time spent on haircuts, we must limit the permissible type of hair styles; bureaucrats begin to split hairs about how many hairs a barber should be allowed to split. A new computerized office of records filled with inspectors and red tape shoots up; some barbers, it seems, are still getting too rich, they must be getting more than their fair share of the national hair, so barbers have to start applying for Certificates of Need in order to buy razors, while peer review boards are established to assess every stylist's work, both the dishonest and the overly honest alike, to make sure that no one is too bad or too good or too busy or too unbusy. Etc. In the end, there are lines of wretched customers waiting for their chance to be routinely scalped by bored, hog-tied haircutters, some of whom remember dreamily the old days when somehow everything was so much better.

Do you think the situation would be improved by having hair-care cooperatives organized by the government?—having them engage in managed competition, managed by the government, in order to buy haircut insurance from companies controlled by the government?

Nobody has the right to the services of any professional individual or group simply because he wants them and desperately needs them.

People Can Afford Health Care

If this is what would happen under government-managed hair care, what else can possibly happen—it is already starting to happen—under the idea of *health* care as a right? Health care in the modern world is a complex, scientific, technological service. How can anybody be born with a right to such a thing?

Under the American system you have a right to health care if you can pay for it, that is, if you can earn it by your own action and effort. But nobody has the right to the services of any professional individual or group simply because he wants them and desperately needs them. The very fact that he needs these services so desperately is the proof that he had better respect the freedom, the integrity, and the rights of the people who provide them.

You have a right to work, not to rob others of the fruits of their work, not to turn others into sacrificial, rightless animals laboring to fulfill your needs.

Some of you may ask here: But can people afford health care on their own? Even leaving aside the present government-inflated medical prices, the answer is: Certainly people can afford it. Where do you think the money is coming from *right now* to pay for it all—where does the government get its fabled unlimited money? Government is not a productive organization; it has no source of wealth other than confiscation of the citizens' wealth, through taxation, deficit financing or the like.

But, you may say, isn't it the "rich" who are really paying the costs of medical care now—the rich, not the broad bulk of the people? As has been proved time and again, there are not enough rich anywhere to make a dent in the government's costs; it is the vast middle class in the U.S. that is the only source of the kind of money that national programs like government health care require. A simple example of this is the fact that all of these new programs rest squarely on the backs not of Big Business, but of small businessmen who are struggling in today's economy merely to stay alive and in existence. Under any socialized regime, it is the "little people" who do most of the paying for it—under the senseless pretext that "the people" can't afford such and such, so the government must take over. If the people of a country truly couldn't afford a certain service—as for example in Somalia—neither, for that very reason, could any government in that country afford it, either.

A Small Minority Need Charity

Some people can't afford medical care in the U.S. But they are necessarily a small minority in a free or even semi-free country. If they were the majority, the country would be an utter bankrupt and could not even think of a national medical program. As to this small minority, in a free country they have to rely solely on private, voluntary charity. Yes, charity, the kindness of the doctors or of the better off—charity, not right, that is not their right to the lives or work of others. And such charity, I may say, was always forthcoming in the past in America. The advocates of Medicaid and Medicare under LBJ [President Lyndon B. Johnson] did not claim that the poor or old in the '60's got bad care; they claimed that it was an affront for anyone to have to depend on charity.

But the fact is: You don't abolish charity by calling it something else. If a person is getting health care for *nothing*, simply because he is breathing, he is still getting charity, whether or not any politician, lobbyist or activist calls it a "right." To call it a Right when the recipient did not earn it is merely to compound the evil. It is charity still—though now extorted by criminal tactics of force, while hiding under a dishonest name.

As with any good or service that is provided by some specific group of men, if you try to make its possession by all a right, you thereby enslave the providers of the service, wreck the service, and end up depriving the very consumers you are supposed to be helping. To call "medical care" a right will merely enslave the doctors and thus destroy the quality of medical care in this country, as socialized medicine has done around the world, wherever it has been tried, including Canada (I was born in Canada and I know a bit about that system first, hand.)

Doctors Under Socialized Medicine

I would like to clarify the point about socialized medicine enslaving the doctors. Let me quote here from an article I wrote a few years ago: "Medicine: The Death of a Profession."

> "In medicine, above all, the mind must be left free. Medical treatment involves countless variables and options that must be taken into account, weighed, and summed up by the doctor's mind and subconscious. Your life depends on the private, inner essence of the doctor's function: it depends on

the input that enters his brain, and on the processing such input receives from him. What is being thrust now into the equation? It is not only objective medical facts any longer. Today, in one form or another, the following also has to enter that brain: 'The DRG [diagnosis-related group] administrator [in effect, the hospital or HMO [health maintenance organization] man trying to control costs] will raise hell if I operate, but the malpractice attorney will have a field day if I don't—and my rival down the street, who heads the local PRO [peer review organization], favors a CAT scan in these cases, I can't afford to antagonize him, but the CON [certificate of need] boys disagree and they won't authorize a CAT scanner for our hospital—and besides the FDA [U.S. Food and Drug Administration] prohibits the drug I should be prescribing, even though it is widely used in Europe, and the IRS [Internal Revenue Service] might not allow the patient a tax deduction for it, anyhow, and I can't get a specialist's advice because the latest Medicare rules prohibit a consultation with this diagnosis, and maybe I shouldn't even take this patient, he's so sick—after all, some doctors are manipulating their slate of patients, they accept only the healthiest ones, so their average costs are coming in lower than mine, and it looks bad for my staff privileges.' Would you like your case to be treated this way—by a doctor who takes into account your objective medical needs *and* the contradictory, unintelligible demands of some ninety different state and Federal government agencies? If you were a doctor could you comply with all of it? Could you plan or work around or deal with the unknowable? But how could you not? Those agencies are real and they are rapidly gaining total power over you and your mind and your patients.

In this kind of nightmare world, if and when it takes hold fully, thought is helpless; no one can decide by rational means what to do. A doctor either obeys the loudest authority—*or* he tries to sneak by unnoticed, bootlegging some good health care occasionally *or*, as so many are doing now, he simply gives up and quits the field."

An End to Quality Medicine

Any mandatory and comprehensive plan will finish off quality medicine in this country—because it will finish off the medical profession. It will deliver doctors bound hands and feet to the mercies of the bureaucracy.

The only hope—for the doctors, for their patients, for all of us—is for the doctors to assert a *moral* principle. I mean: to assert their own personal individual rights—their real rights in this issue—their right to their lives, their liberty, their property, *their* pursuit of happiness. The Declaration of Independence applies to the medical profession too. We must reject the idea that doctors are slaves destined to serve others at the behest of the state.

Doctors, Ayn Rand wrote, are not servants of their patients. They are "traders, like everyone else in a free society, and they should bear that title proudly, considering the crucial importance of the services they offer."

We must reject the idea that doctors are slaves destined to serve others at the behest of the state.

The battle against socialized medicine depends on the doctors speaking out against it—not only on practical grounds, but, first of all, on moral grounds. The doctors must defend themselves and their own interests as a matter of solemn justice, upholding a moral principle, the first moral principle: self-preservation.

Social Security Should Be Eliminated

Alex Epstein

Alex Epstein is an analyst at the Ayn Rand Center for Individual Rights, focusing on business issues.

August 14 [2008] marks Social Security's 73rd birthday—placing it eight years past standard retirement age. But, despite the program's $10-trillion-plus dollar shortfall, no politician dares to suggest that this disastrous program be phased out and retired; all agree on one absolute: Social Security must be saved. While the program may have financial problems, virtually everyone believes that some form of mandatory government-run retirement program is morally necessary.

But is it?

Subject to Government Whim

Social Security is commonly portrayed as benefiting most, if not all, Americans by providing them "risk-free" financial security in old age.

This is a fraud.

Under Social Security, lower- and middle-class individuals are forced to pay a significant portion of their gross income—approximately 12 percent—for the alleged purpose of securing their retirement. That money is not saved or invested, but transferred directly to the program's current beneficiaries—with the "promise" that when current taxpayers get old, the income of future taxpayers will be transferred to them. Since this scheme creates no wealth, any benefits one person receives in excess of his payments necessarily come at the expense of others.

Under Social Security, every aspect of the government's "promise" to provide financial security is at the mercy of political whim. The government can change how much of an individual's money it takes—it has increased the payroll tax 17 times since 1935. The government can spend his money on anything it wants—observe the long-time practice of spending any annual Social Security surplus on other entitlement programs. The government can change when (and therefore if) it chooses to pay him benefits and how much they consist of—witness the current proposals to raise the age cutoff or lower future benefits. Under Social Security, whether an individual gets twice as much from others as was taken from him, or half as much, or nothing at all, is entirely at the discretion of politicians. He cannot count on Social Security for anything—except a massive drain on his income.

How much, when, and in what form one should provide for retirement is highly individual—and is properly left to the individual's free judgment and action.

The Irrational and Irresponsible

If Social Security did not exist—if the individual were free to use that 12 percent of his income as he chose—his ability to better his future would be incomparably greater. He could save for his retirement with a diversified, long-term, productive investment in stocks or bonds. Or he could reasonably choose not to devote all 12 percent to retirement. He might plan to work far past the age of 65. He might plan to live more comfortably when he is young and more modestly in old age. He might choose to invest in his own productivity through additional education or starting a business.

How much, when, and in what form one should provide for retirement is highly individual—and is properly left to the individual's free judgment and action. Social Security deprives the young of this freedom, and thus makes them less able to plan for the future, less able to provide for their retirement, less able to buy homes, less able to enjoy their most vital years, less able to invest in themselves. And yet Social Security's advocates continue to push it as moral. Why?

The answer lies in the program's ideal of "universal coverage"—the idea that, as a *New York Times* editorial preached, "all old people must have the dignity of financial security"—regardless of how irresponsibly they have acted. On this premise, since some would not save adequately on their own, everyone must be forced into some sort of "guaranteed" collective plan—no matter how irrational. Observe that Social Security's wholesale harm to those who would use their income responsibly is justified in the name of those who would not. The rational and responsible are shackled and throttled for the sake of the irrational and irresponsible.

End Social Security

Those who wish to devote their wealth to saving the irresponsible from the consequences of their own actions should be free to do so through private charity, but to loot the savings of untold millions of innocent, responsible, hard-working young people in the name of such a goal is a monstrous injustice.

Social Security in any form is morally irredeemable. We should be debating, not how to save Social Security, but how to end it—how to phase it out so as to best protect both the rights of those who have paid into it, and those who are forced to pay for it today. This will be a painful task. But it will make possible a world in which Americans enjoy far greater freedom to secure their own futures.

Government Intervention in the Capitalist System Is Immoral

Arthur C. Brooks

Arthur C. Brooks is president of the American Enterprise Institute for Public Policy Research. He is the author of Who Really Cares *and* Gross National Happiness: Why Happiness Matters for America—and How We Can Get More of It.

There is a major cultural schism developing in America. But it's not over abortion, same-sex marriage or home schooling, as important as these issues are. The new divide centers on free enterprise—the principle at the core of American culture.

Ethical Populism

Despite President Barack Obama's early personal popularity, we can see the beginnings of this schism in the "tea parties" that have sprung up around the country. In these grass-roots protests, hundreds of thousands of ordinary Americans have joined together to make public their opposition to government deficits, unaccountable bureaucratic power, and a sense that the government is too willing to prop up those who engaged in corporate malfeasance and mortgage fraud.

The data support the protesters' concerns. In a publication with the ironic title, "A New Era of Responsibility," the president's budget office reveals average deficits of 4.7% in the five years after this recession is over. The Congressional Budget Office predicts $9.3 trillion in new debt over the coming decade.

Arthur C. Brooks, "The Real Culture War Is Over Capitalism: Tea Parties, 'Ethical Populism,' and the Moral Case Against Redistribution," *Wall Street Journal*, April 30, 2009, p. A15. Copyright © 2009 Dow Jones & Company, Inc. All rights reserved. Reproduced by permission of the author.

And what investments justify our leaving this gargantuan bill for our children and grandchildren to pay? Absurdities, in the view of many—from bailing out General Motors and the United Auto Workers to building an environmentally friendly Frisbee golf course in Austin, Texas. On behalf of corporate welfare, political largess and powerful special interests, government spending will grow continuously in the coming years as a percentage of the economy—as will tax collections.

Still, the tea parties are not based on the cold wonkery of budget data. They are based on an "ethical populism." The protesters are homeowners who didn't walk away from their mortgages, small business owners who don't want corporate welfare and bankers who kept their heads during the frenzy and don't need bailouts. They were the people who were doing the important things right—and who are now watching elected politicians reward those who did the important things wrong.

Americans Prefer Capitalism

Voices in the media, academia, and the government will dismiss this ethical populism as a fringe movement—maybe even dangerous extremism. In truth, free markets, limited government, and entrepreneurship are still a majoritarian taste. In March 2009, the Pew Research Center asked people if we are better off "in a free market economy even though there may be severe ups and downs from time to time." Fully 70% agreed, versus 20% who disagreed.

Free enterprise is culturally mainstream, for the moment. Asked in a Rasmussen poll conducted this month [April 2009] to choose the better system between capitalism and socialism, 13% of respondents over 40 chose socialism. For those under 30, this percentage rose to 33%. (Republicans were 11 times more likely to prefer capitalism than socialism; Democrats were almost evenly split between the two systems.)

The government has been abetting this trend for years by exempting an increasing number of Americans from federal taxation. My colleague Adam Lerrick showed in these pages last year [in an article published in the *Wall Street Journal* in 2008] that the percentage of American adults who have no federal income-tax liability will rise to 49% from 40% under Mr. Obama's tax plan. Another 11% will pay less than 5% of their income in federal income taxes and less than $1,000 in total.

It is a moral issue to confiscate more income from the minority simply because the government can.

To put a modern twist on the old axiom, a man who is not a socialist at 20 has no heart; a man who is still a socialist at 40 either has no head, or pays no taxes. Social Democrats are working to create a society where the majority are net recipients of the "sharing economy." They are fighting a culture war of attrition with economic tools. Defenders of capitalism risk getting caught flat-footed with increasingly antiquated arguments that free enterprise is a Main Street pocketbook issue. Progressives are working relentlessly to see that it is not.

Government Redistribution Is Immoral

Advocates of free enterprise must learn from the growing grass-roots protests, and make the moral case for freedom and entrepreneurship. They have to declare that it is a moral issue to confiscate more income from the minority simply because the government can. It's also a moral issue to lower the rewards for entrepreneurial success, and to spend what we don't have without regard for our children's future.

Enterprise defenders also have to define "fairness" as protecting merit and freedom. This is more intuitively appealing to Americans than anything involving forced redistribution. Take public attitudes toward the estate tax, which only a few (who leave estates in the millions of dollars) will ever pay, but which two-thirds of Americans believe is "not fair at all," according to a 2009 Harris poll. Millions of ordinary citizens believe it is unfair for the government to be predatory—even if the prey are wealthy.

Political strategy aside, intellectual organizations like my own have a constructive role in the coming cultural conflict. As policymakers offer a redistributionist future to a fearful nation and a new culture war simmers, we must respond with tangible, enterprise-oriented policy alternatives. For example, it is not enough to point out that nationalized health care will make going to the doctor about as much fun as a trip to the department of motor vehicles. We need to offer specific, market-based reform solutions.

This is an exhilarating time for proponents of freedom and individual opportunity. The last several years have brought malaise, in which the "conservative" politicians in power paid little more than lip service to free enterprise. Today, as in the late 1970s, we have an administration, Congress and media-academic complex openly working to change American culture in ways that most mainstream Americans will not like. Like the [President Jimmy] Carter era, this adversity offers the first opportunity in years for true cultural renewal.

Organizations to Contact

The editors have compiled the following list of organizations concerned with the issues debated in this book. The descriptions are derived from materials provided by the organizations. All have publications or information available for interested readers. The list was compiled on the date of publication of the present volume; the information provided here may change. Be aware that many organizations take several weeks or longer to respond to inquiries, so allow as much time as possible.

American Enterprise Institute for Public Policy Research (AEI)
1150 17th St. NW, Washington, DC   20036
(202) 862-5800 • fax: (202) 862-7177
e-mail: info@aei.org
Web site: www.aei.org

The American Enterprise Institute for Public Policy Research is a private, nonpartisan, nonprofit institution dedicated to research and education about issues of government, politics, economics, and social welfare. AEI sponsors research and publishes materials designed to defend the principles and improve the institutions of American freedom and democratic capitalism. AEI publishes *The American*, a bimonthly magazine.

Ayn Rand Institute (ARI)
2121 Alton Pkwy., Suite 250, Irvine, CA   92606-4926
(949) 222-6550 • fax: (949) 222-6558
Web site: www.aynrand.org

The Ayn Rand Institute seeks to spearhead a cultural renaissance in an attempt to reverse the anti-reason, anti-individualism, anti-freedom, anti-capitalist trends it perceives in today's culture. ARI works to introduce young people to Ayn Rand's novels, to support scholarship and research based on her ideas, and to promote the principles of reason, rational self-interest, individual rights, and laissez-faire capitalism to the widest possible audience. The institute publishes information on objectivism and about Ayn Rand, including "Capitalism: The Unknown Ideal."

Cato Institute

1000 Massachusetts Ave. NW, Washington, DC   20001-5403
(202) 842-0200 • fax: (202) 842-3490
Web site: www.cato.org

The Cato Institute is a public policy research foundation dedicated to limiting the role of government, protecting individual liberties, and promoting free markets. The Cato Institute works to originate, advocate, promote, and disseminate applicable policy proposals that create free, open, and civil societies in the United States and throughout the world. Among the Cato Institute's publications is the *Cato Policy Report*, which includes articles such as "Capitalism and Human Nature."

Center for the Advancement of Capitalism

PO Box 221462, Chantilly, VA   20153-1462
e-mail: info@capitalismcenter.org
Web site: www.capitalismcenter.org

The Center for the Advancement of Capitalism is dedicated to advancing individual rights and economic freedom, and it engages in legal advocacy and business advocacy in support of capitalistic principles. Numerous essays are available at the organization's Web site, including "The Moral Basis of Capitalism."

Economic Policy Institute (EPI)

1333 H St. NW, Suite 300, East Tower
Washington, DC   20005-4707
(202) 775-8810 • fax: (202) 775-0819
e-mail: epi@epi.org
Web site: www.epi.org

The Economic Policy Institute is a nonprofit Washington, D.C., think tank that seeks to broaden the discussion about economic policy to include the interests of low- and middle-income workers. EPI briefs policy makers at all levels of government; provides technical support to national, state, and local activists and community organizations; testifies before national, state, and local legislatures; and provides information to the print and electronic media. EPI publishes books, studies, issue briefs, popular education materials, and other publications, among which is the biennially published *State of Working America.*

Institute for America's Future (IAF)

1825 K St. NW, Suite 400, Washington, DC   20006
(202) 955-5665 • fax: (202) 955-5606
Web site: institute.ourfuture.org

The Institute for America's Future works to equip Americans with the tools and information needed to drive issues into the national debate, challenge failed conservative policies, and build support for the progressive vision of a government that is on the side of working people. Working with a network of scholars, activists, and leaders across the country, IAF develops policy ideas, educational materials, and outreach programs. IAF publications include "The Financial Crisis and Crony Capitalism."

Socialist Alternative

PO Box 150457, Brooklyn, NY   11215
(718) 207-4037
e-mail: info@socialistalternative.org
Web site: www.socialistalternative.org

The Socialist Alternative is a national organization fighting against the global capitalist system. Socialist Alternative campaigns for the building of a workers' party to represent the interests of workers, youth, and the environment against what they see as the two parties of big business. Among the publications available on the organization's Web site is the paper, "Why You Should Be a Socialist."

Bibliography

Books

Brian C. Anderson — *Democratic Capitalism and Its Discontents*. Wilmington, DE: ISI Books, 2007.

Dean Baker — *The Conservative Nanny State: How the Wealthy Use the Government to Stay Rich and Get Richer.* Washington, DC: Center for Economic and Policy Research, 2006.

Benjamin R. Barber — *Con$umed: How Markets Corrupt Children, Infantilize Adults, and Swallow Citizens Whole.* New York: W.W. Norton, 2007.

John C. Bogle — *The Battle for the Soul of Capitalism.* New Haven, CT: Yale University Press, 2006.

Thomas G. Donlan — *The World of Wealth: How Capitalism Turns Profits into Progress.* Upper Saddle River, NJ: FT Press, 2008.

Jeffry A. Frieden — *Global Capitalism: Its Fall and Rise in the Twentieth Century.* New York: W.W. Norton, 2007.

David Gratzer — *The Cure: How Capitalism Can Save American Health Care.* New York: Encounter Books, 2006.

Naomi Klein   *The Shock Doctrine: The Rise of Disaster Capitalism*. New York: Metropolitan Books/Henry Holt, 2007.

John R. Lott Jr.   *Freedomnomics: Why the Free Market Works and Other Half-Baked Theories Don't*. Washington, DC: Regnery Publishing, 2007.

Robert P. Murphy   *The Politically Incorrect Guide to Capitalism*. Washington, DC: Regnery Publishing, 2007.

Richard A. Posner   *A Failure of Capitalism: The Crisis of '08 and the Descent into Depression*. Cambridge, MA: Harvard University Press, 2009.

Robert B. Reich   *Supercapitalism: The Transformation of Business, Democracy, and Everyday Life*. New York: Alfred A. Knopf, 2008.

Jay W. Richards   *Money, Greed, and God: Why Capitalism Is the Solution and Not the Problem*. New York: HarperOne, 2009.

Michael Shermer   *The Mind of the Market: Compassionate Apes, Competitive Humans, and Other Tales from Evolutionary Economics*. New York: Times Books, 2007.

Thomas Sowell   *Applied Economics: Thinking Beyond Stage One*. New York: Basic Books, 2009.

Thomas E. Woods Jr.   *Meltdown: A Free-Market Look at Why the Stock Market Collapsed, the Economy Tanked, and Government Bailouts Will Make Things Worse.* Washington, DC: Regnery Publishing, 2009.

Periodicals

Ralph Atkins   "Europe Wary of US-Style Capitalism," *Financial Times,* September 23, 2007.

David Boaz   "Bush and Obama Opt for Corporatism over Freewheeling Capitalist Economy," *Investors Business Daily,* December 17, 2008.

Donald Boudreaux   "The Case for Neglecting Global Warming," *Pittsburgh Tribune-Review,* August 13, 2006.

Jonathan Chait   "Dead Left," *New Republic,* July 30, 2008.

Mona Charen   "Stand Up for Capitalism!" *National Review Online,* March 6, 2009. www.nationalreview.com.

Barbara Ehrenreich and Bill Fletcher Jr.   "Reimagining Socialism," *Nation,* March 23, 2009.

Larry Elder   "Is Capitalism on the Ropes?" Creators.com, September 25, 2008. www.creators.com.

Anthony Faiola   "The End of American Capitalism?" *Washington Post*, October 10, 2008.

Erik Gartzke   "Future Depends on Capitalizing on Capitalist Peace," *Windsor Star*, October 1, 2005.

David Gratzer   "For Health Care Woes, A Capitalism Prescription," *Washington Post*, October 25, 2006.

Kevin A. Hassett   "Cronies Against Capitalism," *National Review*, March 24, 2008.

Austin Hill   "Is Barack Obama the 'Moral Alternative' to Capitalism?" Townhall.com, April 5, 2009. www.townhall.com.

Paul Hsieh   "Mandatory Health Insurance: Wrong for Massachusetts, Wrong for America," *Objective Standard*, Fall 2008.

Investor's Business Daily   "Capitalism Lives!" January 23, 2008.

Naomi Klein   "Disaster Capitalism: The New Economy of Catastrophe," *Harper's*, October 2007.

Mark Levinson   "Worse Than You Thought," *Dissent*, Spring 2005. www.dissentmagazine.org.

David Limbaugh   "Memo to Capitalists: Be Very Afraid," Townhall.com, May 8, 2009. www.townhall.com.

Brink Lindsey "The Curious Problem of Having More Than You Need," *Wall Street Journal*, April 3, 2007.

Johan Norberg "The Klein Doctrine: The Rise of Disaster Polemics," Cato Institute Briefing Paper no. 102, May 14, 2008.

Richard D. North "Rich Is Beautiful," *Cato Policy Report*, November/December 2005.

Laurent Pinsolle, translated by Leslie Thatcher "Is Free-Market Fundamentalism Immoral?" *Truthout*, January 3, 2009. www.truthout.org.

Alan Reynolds "Is Capitalism Dead? Yes," NPR.org, March 11, 2009. www.npr.org.

Michael Schuman "Why Government Intervention Won't Last," *Time*, November 25, 2008.

Amartya Sen "Capitalism Beyond the Crisis," *New York Review of Books*, March 26, 2009.

Judy Shelton "Capitalism Needs a Sound-Money Foundation," *Wall Street Journal*, February 12, 2009.

Brian Simpson "Gold and a Free Market: The Solutions to Our Financial Crisis," *Capitalism Magazine*, October 31, 2008. www.capmag.com.

Thomas Sowell "Words Versus Realities," *Capitalism Magazine*, April 21, 2009. www.capmag.com.

Michael D. Stroup   "Which Is More Important for
Women, Capitalism or Democracy?"
National Center for Policy Analysis,
no. 621, July 14, 2008. www.ncpa.org.

Stefan Theil   "Europe's Philosophy of Failure,"
Foreign Policy, January/February
2008.

Michael Walzer   "A Note on Greed: Who Is Really to
Blame for the Financial Troubles?"
Dissent, September 29, 2008.
www.dissentmagazine.org.

Marianne
Meed Ward   "It's Time for a Real Debate on
Capitalism," *Toronto Sun*, September
21, 2008.

Washington Post   "Is Capitalism Dead?: The Market
That Failed Was Not Exactly Free,"
October 20, 2008.

Alan M. Webber   "Giving the Poor the Business," *USA
Today*, May 21, 2008.

David Wessel   "Bankruptcy Is Vital to Capitalism,"
Wall Street Journal, April 2, 2009.

Will Wilkinson   "Obama's Self-Immolating
Capitalism," *The Week*, March 19,
2009. www.theweek.com.

Walter Williams   "Capitalism and the Financial Crisis,"
Jewish World Review, November 5,
2008.

Lin Zinser and
Paul Hsieh   "Moral Health Care vs. 'Universal
Health Care,'" *Objective Standard*,
Winter 2007–2008.

Index

A

Aceh (Indonesia), 102, 103, 109
Ackermann, Josef, 128
Afghanistan, 38, 62, 103, 106–107
Africa, 39, 78, 79, 100
African Americans, 93
Aggressive capitalism, 22–24
Altruism
    bailouts and, 168
    Federal Reserve and, 166, 169
    government intervention and, 163–164, 167–168
    housing market and, 164–165
    moral hazard from, 165–167
    Obama, Barack and, 71
    paying for, 168
    rejection of, 169
    sacrifice and, 32–34
    self-interest and, 30–31, 35, 169
American Bill of Rights, 87
American Enterprise Institute, 107
American Investment Group (AIG), 159, 161
American Society of Engineers, 92
Anti-capitalism, 52, 53, 110–111
Argentina, 81, 112–113, 191
Aristide, Jean-Bertrand, 107
Aristotle (Greek philosopher), 38, 43
Asia, 78, 88, 89, 111, 138
Australia, 111–112
Authoritarian rule, 19–20, 90, 112, 178

B

Bailouts
    altruism and, 168
    democracy and, 83–84
    global financial crisis and, 160, 173
    government spending on, 143
    leveraging and, 134–135
    as moral hazard, 156–158, 162
    reallocation of capital and, 155
    under responsible capitalism, 27–28, 63, 67
Bakunin, Mikhail, 37
Bank of America, 83
Bank of New York Mellon, 83
Barber, Benjamin R., 66–72
Becker, Gary, 37
Beethoven, Ludwig van, 40
Belgium, 45
Bentham, Jeremy, 37
Bevan, Aneurin, 181
Biddle, Craig, 26–36
Blair, Tony, 112
Bond transactions, 124–126
Bourgeois capitalism, 39–42
Bourgeois virtues, 44, 45–46
Brandeis, Louis, 76
Brederode, Henry, 46
British Journal of Political Science (online journal), 112
British National Health, 178, 181
Brook, Yaron, 170–173
Brooks, Arthur C., 206–209
Bush, George H. W., 61
Bush, George W. (administration)

L

M